IDENTITY THEFT

The Ultimate Protection: Defending Who You Are

by

Terence B. Lester

Identity is the foundation and building block of our life's purpose.

Identity Theft
The Ultimate Protection: Defending Who You Are

© 2009 by Terence B. Lester

All rights reserved. No part of this book may be reproduced, stored in a retrieval system, or transmitted in any form or by any means—electronic, mechanical, photocopy, recording, or otherwise—without written permission of the publisher, except for brief quotations in printed reviews.

Scripture quotations marked KJV are taken from the King James Version.

Scripture quotations marked NIV are taken from the Holy Bible, New International Version®. Copyright © 1973, 1978, 1984 by International Bible Society. Used by permission of Zondervan. All rights reserved.

Scripture quotations marked NKJV are taken from the New King James Version®. Copyright © 1982 by Thomas Nelson, Inc. Used by permission. All rights reserved.

ISBN- 978-0-692-00333-6

Printed in the United States of America

DEDICATION

~

I dedicate this book to my beautiful daughter, Zion Joy Lester, who is only five months old. Since you were born, you have become a constant encouragement that pushes me every day of my life. I love you with all my heart because you are the apple of my eye. My prayer is that you find God at an early age, build a relationship with Him, and protect the identity He has given you. Apart from Him, life is meaningless.

I love you,

Dad

ACKNOWLEDGMENTS

~

My whole being is filled with praise for the many individuals who have blessed my life. I dedicate this book first and foremost to *God.* Without Him in my life, none of this is possible. I love Him for what He's doing in my life as well as in the world.

Special thanks have been earned by one of the most supportive people in my life, my wife, *Cecilia L. Lester.* I want you to know that you are my heart. I love you for who you are and what you bring to our marriage. To my mother, *Connie Walker*, and stepfather, *Dewitt Walker*, thanks for always pushing Cecilia and me to be the best we can be. To my dad, *Tyrone Lester*, thanks for instilling in me courage to fight for my dreams. To *Ashely Lester*, my sister, who means the world to me, I love you and believe in you. To my nephew, *Carmello O'Neal*, you're going to become a great man one day.

To our pastor, *Bishop Dale C. Bronner*, thank you for your messages that inspire our family to keep shooting for the stars. Special thanks to *Patrick Remy*, *Isaac Walters*, *Latasha Bradford*, and *Tiffany Linen* for your timely words of encouragement. They helped me to produce a work of God.

To *Marquis* and *Dalina Phelps*, *Harvey Strickland*, *Kurston Strictland*, *Gloria Spence*, *Darrell Fitzpatrick*, *Vinod Thomas*, *Takeisha Paster* (social work student at the University of Alabama), *Marsha* and *Jim Brown*, *Kenya* and

Nick Ross, ***Craige Frazier***, ***Roy Currie***, ***Marquis*** and ***Aisha Alston***, ***Uncle Frank Marshall***, ***Martize Spearman***, ***Dexter*** and ***Quiana Culbreath***, ***Ron*** and ***Marie Eason***, ***Barbra*** and ***Darrell Combs***, thank you all for adding value to Cecilia's, Zion's, and my lives. It has been said, "You can tell a lot about a person from the people who surround him or her." Because you all are around us, our lives have been enriched immensely. We love you all.

To all my family, my wife's family, and all the added family God has given me, thanks for the constant support you give to Cecilia, Zion, and me.

Thanks for all of your prayers and encouragement.

TABLE OF CONTENTS

FOREWORD ix

INTRODUCTION 1

I DISCOVERY: THE UNVEILING OF IDENTITY 3

    DISCOVERY 4

    IDENTITY THEFT DEFINED 8

    DISCOVERING IDENTITY 15

II AN ALL-INCLUSIVE OPPORTUNITY 20

    PERSONAL PROTECTION PLAN 21

    FAMILY PROTECTION PLAN 23

III TRUE-LIFE STORIES 26

    CASE 1: DREAMS BLOWN BY ILL WINDS 27

    CASE 2: DIMINISHED FAITH ALONG THE WAY ... 33

    CASE 3: A TOUGH ROAD FOR A SINGLE DAD 37

    CASE 4: WHEN CURSES STALK YOUR 43
    BLOODLINE

IV SAFEGUARD ALERT: PROTECTION FEATURES ... 47

    PROTECTION FROM DIS-TRACK-TIONS 48

PROTECTION AGAINST YOUR PAST 52

PROTECTION AGAINST UNFORGIVINGNESS 56

PROTECTION AGAINST LACK OF FOCUS 62

PROTECTION AGAINST NAÏVETÉ 66

PROTECTION AGAINST COMPROMISE 71

PROTECTION AGAINST EXCUSES 76

PROTECTION AGAINST DEVALUATION 81

PROTECTION FROM OBSTACLES 84

PROTECTION FROM COMPLAINTS 90

PROTECTION FROM CURSE WORDS 93

PROTECTION AGAINST PROCRASTINATION 97

   A Lesson on Life's Highway: There Is a Reason! 102

   Roadwork: Taking the Time to Work Your Path 104

PROTECTION AGAINST SELF-SERVING 106

PHILOSOPHY, MISUSE OF POWER, AND POSITION

PROTECTION AGAINST WRONG 116
ASSOCIATIONS

PROTECTION AGAINST THE ILLUSION 125

OF PROSPERITY (Status) AND POSSESSIONS

(Materialism)

PROTECTION AGAINST ARROGANT PRIDE..........133

AND PROGRESS

    Victim and Predator 133

    The Scab and the Scar 134

    In Due Season..136

THE MAINTAINING OF YOUR 140

PROTECTION

SUMMARY 144

ABOUT THE AUTHOR..150

FOREWORD

~

Every so often God raises up a voice to speak to the common man about the matters that are closest to His heart. Terence Lester is such a man. God has bestowed an ability upon Terence to address issues that the common person is facing today. In prophetic fashion, he brings to light the struggles we face and the destructive effect these struggles have upon our lives if we do not overcome them.

In this book, ***Identity Theft***, we find more help in living God's plan for our lives. Terence identifies those forces in life that endeavor to undermine God's creative order and purpose in our lives. Genesis 1-3 spells out clearly our nature and what God intends for us. Soon thereafter, Satan entered and stole the identities of our first parents. Since then, the whole world has been struggling to find themselves. None of us are immune.

Satan stole Adam's and Eve's identities by undermining their relationships with God through casting doubt in their hearts concerning God's word. Furthermore, the Devil robbed them of their innocence by tempting them to sin and discovering in practice the knowledge of good and evil. They did not become as God but became much less than God intended them to be. So great was their loss that they attempted to hide from God's presence and to cover their nakedness with fig leaves. All of our human attempts to find our identities without Christ have been fig leaves over our naked hearts and lives.

Identity Theft is a book that will help you find your identity, protect your identity, and preserve your identity against future loss. It will help you find your true identity in Christ and how that identity can be preserved through the spiritual weapons provided for us in Scripture. It will help you identify and use these weapons to ward off those who seek to undermine your relationship with God, and it will help you strengthen your faith in our Lord Jesus Christ so that you can be a champion for Christ's church.

I heartedly recommend reading this book and thank the Lord that He has given Terence Lester the insight and desire to make this book a help to our community. He will help you prevent identity theft.

Dr. Alex D. Montoya
Pastor of The First Fundamental Bible Church
Author of ***Preaching with Passion***
January 27, 2009

INTRODUCTION

~

"Identity is finding your purpose in life and not giving up."
-Terence B. Lester

Normally when you hear the phrase "identity theft," you think about someone having the audacity to take advantage of the photo and document you hate to show people, a piece of ID you are forced to reveal, such as your driving credentials or work pass. Maybe you think about the general description one uses to identify you from another person. You may think it is an employee badge or card you swipe to access an account in which you deposit funds. In other words, many individuals relate identity to things that are tangible rather than intangible. However, I believe there are examples of identity theft that bring more chaos to our lives than the loss of a driver's license, employee badges, or debit cards.

Think about the countless times you have misplaced your ID when you really needed it most. For a period of time, your activity was restricted, including your ability to write checks and to make certain purchases. You may have been denied access to other privileges. Now imagine not losing a piece of plastic but looking up one day to find you have actually misplaced who you are. What if the fumbling around, the hustle and bustle, and the obstacles of life have caused you to misplace yourself?

Whether we are aware of it or not, the greatest thing that we can misplace is our identities. Who we are and what we become matters more than anything else in life. Identity is the foundation, the building block, of each individual's life purpose. It is also the key to the door of fulfillment. It is only when we find ourselves internally that we begin to determine who we really are.

I'll never forget walking through a well-known chain store in search of a present for my nephew. I went throughout the toy section looking for the perfect gift for Christmas. The search brought back so many memories. I revisited my childhood as I observed some of the same toys that brought joy to me as a child as well as others new to the market. I could not forget those thousand-piece puzzles! Even though I absolutely hated them, I received so many puzzles as gifts. I thought that people gave them to other people because they were too cheap to buy nice gifts.

As I think about puzzles today, I realize the significance of each piece, even when it has one thousand pieces. You actually need all of the pieces to appreciate the effort and the result totally. Sometimes we try to force a piece into a space that does not fit. Likewise, in our lives, it is awkward to force a section or a piece that does not fit. Yet many people spend many years of their lives gathering insignificant pieces or sections that do not fit the image that God has designed for their life portraits.

In this book, I want to show you how to discover your identity and protect it from the sixteen identity thieves that have the potential to steal our identities each day and steal our sense of who we truly are and the persons God wants us to become.

I

DISCOVERY

THE UNVEILING OF IDENTITY

Man began his quest to the moon because he could see it in the distance. Natural curiosity gave birth to a multibillion-dollar space program. Discovery can be a wonderful thing. Lack of discovery can be just as dangerous. To go through life and miss the privilege of God-given identity is a tragedy!

What is this thing called "identity" and how can anyone or anything manage to steal it from us? We now embark on a journey of discovery!

DISCOVERY!

~

"Inside, we discover who we are."
-Terence B. Lester

Deep within every single soul there lies specific purpose. Sometimes this purpose is hidden or undiscovered. It is up to the individual to uncover the real purpose for his or her life. The most important factor in discovering that purpose is to connect with one's true identity. However, usually there will be obstacles or barriers along the way.

Before I started writing this book, circumstances seemed to indicate that it just would not happen. I had just been laid off from my job, I owed thousands of dollars to creditors, and my car was not running. And, if that was not enough, I had unpaid student loans for a degree that I had yet to use! Nothing was going right for me! It was as though every discouraging spirit in the universe had been dispatched to take me under. I remember the sequence of events far too well.

First, there was a call from the main office on a Friday afternoon. The voice on the other end said, "May I speak to Terence Lester?"

"This is he," I said.

"I apologize, but your assignment has been cancelled, and you don't have to report to work any longer." She stated this in a quite matter-of-fact tone.

I was devastated! How could I ever get back on my feet? I was planning to get married soon. How could I take care of a wife? How would I take care of myself?

I began to question my purpose, destiny, and support system. I wondered if I was destined to be successful or well on the way to being a participant in the world's greatest pretense. Either way, I did not feel good about myself or the way things were going. It's funny how bad times cause us to look into the mirror and see someone who doesn't belong. We see a reflection not of who we are but of who we will become—if we lose our identities.

That brings me to the title of this book, ***Identity Theft***. I now realize that I almost allowed an unseen enemy to steal my image, my name, and my spiritual domain. All of these factors go into the making of the persons that we are to become.

I actually believe that one of the chief goals of the enemy is to take over our identities so that we will not be able to walk into our destinies and realize the fulfillment that God has predestined for all of us. My life was a classic example.

In an earlier book, ***U-Turn***, I shared the story of my troubled childhood and adolescence. It was apparent to me that I was marked by God from the beginning for greatness and sought after, at the same time, by the Devil for destruction.

For a while in my life, I worked several different jobs, none of which provided an opportunity to display my true gifts, talents, and abilities. I knew there was purpose assigned to my life; however, I could not understand how these gifts could ever prosper and grow. I was overwhelmed, busy doing things that really didn't matter. This was a frustrating place to be in life. I could not go on like this and be content. There was something deep down inside that gnawed at my very existence. I felt as though there was a serious illness plaguing my body that would not let go. I did not like this feeling in any way. My soul longed for something deeper and more rewarding.

> One of the chief goals of the enemy is to take over our identities so that we will not be able to walk into our destinies and realize the fulfillment that God has predestined for all of us.

For my entire life, I have known that my purpose included standing before thousands of people and bringing a message of encouragement and hope. I have known that I am to write and to circulate books around the country. I had dreams of transporting books (whose words came straight from my heart) and delivering them to waiting audiences who had also experienced much of the disappointment that I had gone through but could not find their way out. I've known for many years that I am to help them.

I experienced days of extreme highs when I felt on top of the world and just wanted to be on the way to rescuing the lost. Then there were days when things were not going so well, and I just wanted to give up because nothing that I saw in the natural supported my dream and purpose. It's hard to feel as though you are out to rescue anyone when you don't even have a car to ride in or a dime in your pocket. Somehow I came to the realization that dreams are lived, not achieved.

I was soon to learn that everything that I went through was simply a dress rehearsal and preparation in shaping my identity. Neither rehearsals, learning lines, stage fright, nor any of the other mishaps during this time were without merit; in fact, they added substantially to my life journey. Even the mistakes and the valley moments helped to shape my identity.

Now is as good a time as any to decide that you too will not fall victim to the pitfalls of error, discouragement, depression, low self-esteem, or adversity. All of these are generals in an army whose specialty is stealing one's identity. They fight a fierce battle. **Hold on! Don't let them invade your fort!**

> Deep within every single soul there lies specific purpose.

Once, our elders cautioned us that, above all else, we had to protect our names. However, we have more than our names to protect. Far more importantly, we must protect our **identities**!

IDENTITY THEFT DEFINED

~

"If Identity is stolen, purpose is distorted."
                                        -*Terence B. Lester*

Statistics indicate that every 3.8 seconds someone becomes an innocent victim of identity theft. It is a troubling matter to know that every 79 seconds a criminal takes advantage of modern technology, going into a computer and stealing another person's life. This can cause problems for that individual for years to come.

Even though it is one of the fastest growing crimes in the United States, affecting nearly one million victims each year, I'd like to address a violation that is much more detrimental to an individual than the loss of a checkbook, credit cards, or a driver's license. Although all of these are unfortunate circumstances, we have some comfort in knowing that there are agencies and procedures in place that address such theft. However, a subtle and more invasive theft involves the literal taking of one's soul and all that it represents. There are no toll-free numbers to provide a quick fix for these occurrences. The answers lie deep within.

I love a quote from Norman Vincent Peale. In *The Power of Positive Thinking*, he noted, "Altogether many people are defeated by the everyday problems of life; they go struggling, perhaps whining through their days with a dull resentment at which they consider the 'bad breaks' life has given them." He added, "You need be defeated only if you are willing to be." I believe that what he is trying to convey is that, no matter how difficult our situations may be or how drastic our circumstances, we should not allow what we are going through to control our identities to the point that we feel inadequate.

I remember having a conversation with my stepfather during lunch one day. We got on the subject of preventing worry from infiltrating our minds. He shared with me the story of a childhood bout with pneumonia that was life threatening. The doctor told his aunt that he was "as good as dead." He related this death sentence to a significant series of unfortunate events over the course of his life, including abandonment by his mother, the death of his father at two weeks old, and his birth defect.

He survived the episode of pneumonia and was successful in spite of the obstacles and disadvantage of not having his parents in his life. He was forced to overcome a lot from the very beginning; yet he survived to become a productive citizen with great leadership responsibilities. A key ingredient in his survival included refusing to focus on the negative or resorting to the comfort of self-pity and worry.

He stated that when he found himself and his true identity, he was able to live his life without worrying or letting anything get to him. He told me that his grandfather used to say that all of the water in the world cannot sink a ship unless it actually gets into the ship. That makes a lot of sense. When we allow our circumstances to get the best of us, they can take us down and distort our identities.

Recognition of your identity is very important because it allows you to be confident even in the roughest times. Blaise Pascal wrote, "Our achievements of today are but the sum total of our thoughts of yesterday. You are today where the thoughts of yesterday have brought you and you will be tomorrow where the thoughts of today take you."

Just imagine a kingdom where birds do not fly, bees do not buzz, fish do not swim, and caterpillars do not crawl. There is nothing as elusive or counterproductive as not living out the life you are called to produce. Sure, it's great to have a six-figure income; but does the job bring any fulfillment or solidify your purpose as a human being? Think about it. I honestly believe that personal unhappiness exists on such a large scale because people are operating outside of their purposes. There is probably nothing more dissatisfying than to float on the ocean of life without a clue as to the final destination. Many people drown in this sea because they fail to put on their lifejackets of **identity**. In fact, they fail to place them on the boat! Please accept a word of caution for surviving this ocean called life: **Don't be found on the oceans of life without this lifejacket!**

Identity is a potent life component that can take you to great heights or usher you to great lows and sadness. Something deeply imbedded within human nature longs to produce the masterpieces we have been commissioned to paint. Until we complete these works through the brushstrokes of our lives, we will always have voids that yearn to be filled.

Even Jesus, the Son of God, was challenged during His life on earth in regards to His purpose and identity. The Master performed magnificently in overcoming the situation.

In the book of Matthew, Jesus had just been baptized by John the Baptist and the spirit descended like a dove. A voice then, in no uncertain terms, confirmed the true identity of Jesus in these words: "**THIS IS** my beloved Son in whom I am well pleased." (Matthew 3:17b NKJV; emphasis added).

Afterwards, Jesus was alone in the wildness and the Devil attempted to invalidate this special distinction and kinship to God Almighty. He taunted Jesus with the words, **"IF you are the Son Of God"** in Matthew 4:1-11 (NKJV; emphasis added).

> *¹Then Jesus was led up by the Spirit into the wilderness to be tempted by the devil. ²And when He had fasted forty days and forty nights, afterward He was hungry. ³Now when the tempter came to Him, he said, **"If You are the Son of God,** command that these stones become bread." ⁴But He answered and said, "It is written, 'Man shall not live by bread alone, but by every word that proceeds from the mouth of God.'" ⁵Then the devil took Him up into the holy city, set Him on the pinnacle of the temple, ⁶and said to Him, **"If You are the Son of God,** throw Yourself down. For it is written: 'He shall give His angels charge over you,' and, 'In their hands they shall bear you up, lest you dash your foot against a stone.'" ⁷Jesus*

*said to him, "It is written again, 'You shall not tempt the LORD your God.'" ⁸Again, the devil took Him up on an exceedingly high mountain, and showed Him all the kingdoms of the world and their glory. ⁹And he said to Him, "All these things I will give You **if You** will fall down and worship me." ¹⁰Then Jesus said to him, "Away with you, Satan! For it is written, 'You shall worship the LORD your God, and Him only you shall serve.'" ¹¹Then the devil left Him, and behold, angels came and ministered to Him.*

Please note that immediately after God affirmed His Son's identity and confirmed His purpose, the enemy began to play games. Isn't it strange that right after you know what you are to do with your life, identify the business you are supposed to start, discover the organization you are supposed to be a part of, find the relationship that you are supposed to have, you are often led into a wilderness? The wilderness is a low, lonely place. When you look up the word *wilderness* in Webster's dictionary, you'll find one definition that states "an empty or pathless area or region." Isn't it amazing how sometimes right after we are called to specific tasks we find ourselves in what seems to be a maze without any defined path?

What really struck my spirit about this particular chapter is how the Devil tempted Jesus right after He was given authority by His Father. Remember, God stated emphatically, "This is my Son"; and while Jesus was in the wilderness, each time the Devil tempted Jesus, he blatantly used the words, "if you . . . if you . . . if you . . . ." The reason this is significant to me is because, when things are not going our way on the journey to purpose, the enemy **will** hurl a conditional and faith-diminishing statement like "if" when God has already said **"this is."**

Every time I've ever faced a negative or plaguing situation, it has almost been as if the Devil is right there taunting me, saying, "You can't do it!" The Devil wants us to think that it is possible that we are not who God says we are. I want you to know that the Devil is a liar and **what God has affirmed and created you to do, you will indeed accomplish!**

This passage in Matthew alone is sufficient reason for writing this book. The greatest spiritual teacher in the universe declared and, more importantly, maintained His identity in the face of adversity. The Devil tempted Him three times, but each time He was confident in knowing

> Isn't it strange that right after you know what you are to do with your life . . . you are often led into a wilderness?

that He indeed belonged to the Father. He was consistent; and, in divine defiance, He told the Devil to flee. And he did! The Bible plainly states that if you resist the Devil, he will flee from you.

Jesus emerged from the wilderness with far greater witness power. He then proceeded with His ministry, consequently touching the whole world. Of course, He encountered other problems on His journey, but He understood that challenges provided the opportunity to do His best.

We should pattern our lives after His example. We should never let others challenge our identities or define who we are. If you feel you have been lured into the wilderness of life, you must meet the enemy head on and **tell** him who you are! Know that God has already claimed you and will help you get right back on track to protect your identity.

Even though I have never been in the military, I've seen in the movies a symbolic bugle call used to announce the beginning of the day. There is another bugle call to signal the end of the day or a time to sleep. In the military, it is important that you are not sleeping during waking hours. As we are reminded in Ecclesiastes, there is a season for all things—a time to sleep and a time to be awake and aware.

I believe that the enemy of this present age is determined to bring about a deep sleep upon God's people so that they will be numb or unaware of the direction they are supposed to move or when they are to move. Evidence can be found in the example of relationships that fail, individuals not facing up to their responsibilities to take care of their families, broken homes, the high rate of incarcerations, and early and tragic deaths of young people. The Devil uses all of these as mere examples of what will happen if we are spiritually asleep during times when we should be awake. When we are asleep, we are vulnerable to invasion, being taken advantage of, and the gross misuse of our **identities**.

DISCOVERING IDENTITY

~

"I believe developing identity has to do with adding the right essentials to your life."
-Terence B. Lester

Identity is formed and created based on our core beliefs. Our belief systems constitute who we are, why we are, and who we can become. For instance, a butterfly cannot take on the identity of a butterfly unless it believes it is no longer a caterpillar. What we believe about ourselves gives us the power to have the metamorphosis we desire and need in our lives. Ralph Waldo Emerson observed, "A person will worship something, have no doubt about that. We may think our tribute is paid in secret in the dark recesses of our hearts, but it will out. That which dominates our imaginations and our thoughts will determine our lives, and our character. Therefore, it behooves us to be careful what we worship, for what we are worshipping we are becoming." In Genesis 1:26-28 (NKJV), God let us know immediately that we were made in His image and likeness:

> [26]*Then God said, "Let Us make man in Our image, according to Our likeness; let them have dominion over the fish of the sea, over the birds of the air, and over the cattle, over all the earth and over every creeping thing that creeps on the earth." [27]So God created man in His own image; in the image of God He created him; male and female He created them. [28]Then God*

blessed them, and God said to them, "Be fruitful and multiply; fill the earth and subdue it; have dominion over the fish of the sea, over the birds of the air, and over every living thing that moves on the earth.

Our identities are always tied to what we are made like—God. God is a limitless, confident, gracious, and peaceful God. If I named all of His names, I would take up this whole book and more. However, when we understand our identities, we must understand them from their original source. In *Handbook of Self and Identity*, Leary and Tangney[*] reported that a psychological identity relates to self-image (a person's mental model of him or herself), self-esteem, and individuation.

> What we believe about ourselves gives us the power to have the metamorphosis we desire.

Some people never have the power to develop into who God wants them to become because they have settled for a contaminated belief system. They have tied their identities to the created instead of the Creator. They have adopted what the enemy has said, not what God has promised. Sadly, most people base their beliefs on tangible exterior things that, when they fail, leave them wondering who they are. Recently, mid-2008, we faced economic devastation when our economy

---

[*] M. R. Leary and J. P. Tangney, *Handbook of Self and Identity* (New York: Guilford Press, 2003).

started to falter. The stock market plummeted without warning; and many people lost millions, even billions, of dollars. Companies went bankrupt, unemployment increased, and foreclosures skyrocketed. People even committed suicide because they lost their assets and money. This alone shows us that when our beliefs are in the wrong place and not founded on the right beliefs and hard times come, we have left room for the adversity and hard times to steal who we are.

From my perspective and life experiences, I have decided that inner identity is made up of four major ingredients:

- Our relationships with God

- Our relationships with ourselves

- Our relationships with our friends

- Our thoughts

Our relationships with God are very important because here we embark upon our ultimate mission (to love our neighbor as we love ourselves) and to find out who we really are. We discover His will not only for us but for mankind as well. Many people never acknowledge God; however, they are left with a void that no earthly possession, person, or prosperity will ever fulfill. Many people missing God in their lives will substitute violence, drugs, sex, anger, and even pride. An early biblical example is the account of Adam and Eve. A perfect relationship and a perfect life were seriously affected when they dishonored a wonderful opportunity to secure their relationships with God through obedience.

Our relationships with ourselves are vitally important because we must believe in ourselves and, more importantly, love ourselves. Many people hate themselves based on their family backgrounds; their size, shape, or race; their economic status or education; or their relationships. However, none of these things has any real power over who we are to become.

Our relationships with friends are important because most people take on at least some of the qualities of their associates—good or bad. Our friends and associates prophesy to our future. Why? Because we are not only what we eat but who we hang around as well. Stagnant personalities, complainers, procrastinators, and people who do not value time add little to our success or accomplishments. If someone is using you only for that person's benefit, then you should evaluate the value or advantage of this association. Is he there for you when you need help? Is she loyal? Is he involved in conversations about you behind your back?

Our thoughts are so powerful that we can shape our days, months, and years with a single moment of mental activity. Our thoughts literally shape the way we see ourselves and the world before us. I remember one of my close friends sharing with me that what we choose to think can slowly reprogram all the ways we have thought in the past. Many times our identities hinge upon the thoughts we have of ourselves, our past thoughts, and our thoughts about our lives. If we allow negative thoughts to invade our minds, we will only produce what we process. Our thoughts are so deeply connected with our attitudes that the right thought can bring us to a state of perfect peace and a negative thought can bring turmoil, worry, and much inner conflict. I think this is probably what Maya Angelou meant when she wrote "I Know Why the Caged Bird Sings." I believe the bird sang because it didn't allow a negative experience to determine what it thought of itself.

Even though shipwrecked, beaten, stripped, imprisoned, and mocked, the apostle Paul always found time to write letters of great magnitude that were both positive and encouraging. Philippians, one of the letters found in the New Testament, is one of my favorites. Included in his powerful testimony, we find the words, "But I want you to know, brethren, that the things which happened to me have actually turned out for the furtherance of the gospel" (Philippians 1:12 NKJV). I admire his courage and self-sacrificial mindset in this passage. In spite of all that he had gone through, he still had an appreciative attitude. Do you think that you could be as positive as Paul if you had a similar set of troubles?

> Our thoughts literally shape the way we see ourselves.

II

AN ALL-INCLUSIVE OPPORTUNITY

It is not God's will that any man, boy, woman, or girl should perish. To proceed as He has planned, it is necessary to first protect our personal identities and then to enable others to do the same.

PERSONAL PROTECTION PLAN

~

"The Lord is my rock and my fortress and my deliverer; My God, my strength, in whom I will trust; My shield and the horn of my salvation, my stronghold."
-Psalms 18:2 (NKJV)

The job I landed after working in a warehouse was that of an in-school suspension teacher. This was far better than being in the warehouse; yet it wasn't what I was destined to do. Even in the midst of being in the wrong place, there were lessons for me to learn. For example, at a meeting of the faculty one afternoon after work, a speaker discussed traditional identity theft. As I watched clips of individuals who shared how their lives had been altered for years as they worked their way out of this serious violation of their privacy, I realized that what I was going through was quite similar. I listened as the woman revealed how criminals target their prey. They look for people who have their guard down, who are naïve, and who don't carefully protect their assets. She was describing what was going on in my life.

When we don't protect what God has given us, it can easily be stolen! How have you protected your dream, gift, talent, or asset that God has given to you?

At the end of the presentation, she distributed folders from her company that outlined a personal protection plan. I examined the various plans beginning with the first level of protection offered. As I looked at protecting myself in the area of identity theft, as most people know it, I also began to look at the parallel experiences in my personal and emotional life. I decided that what I needed to do to stop the wheels from turning in the wrong direction and leaving me open to spiritual identity theft was to lay a strong foundation in three primary areas:

- Prayer

- Focus

- Movement

Prayer gives us the proper connection with God through which He can minister to us through our ups and downs. God provides the foundation of strength because when we are not strong enough, His grace alone gives us the power to trudge on in the face of adversity.

Focus serves to keep us on track because the Devil desires to get our attention and distract us with temptations and superficial pleasures.

Movement is important because, without momentum, we are going absolutely nowhere.

There are a number of ways that we become prey for identity theft. As I mentioned previously, one such device is the power of distraction or, for the purpose of this book, "dis-tracktions." Later in the book, in the Safeguard features, we will discover a new meaning for the word distraction (dis-tracktion) and the reason I have spelled it this particular way.

FAMILY PROTECTION PLAN

~

"The love, protection, and security of a family are life's greatest blessing."
-Terence B. Lester

In addition to the personal plan, the woman with the identity protection program also presented a family protection plan. She went through the problems that all members of the family could encounter as far as this invasion was concerned. We all agreed that this kind of protection was a good thing and that the entire family should be protected.

This carried me back to my childhood. I remembered how a family needs special protection. I remembered how my mother served as a single parent in our household and how hard she worked to keep things going. Because my father had left the family, I was unprotected in a number of ways. It was easy for the enemy to creep in, orchestrate evil works, and present many dis-track-tions. Unfortunately, I fell for many of his devices and temporarily wandered off the right path.

I began quickly to think about my present life, my relationship with Cecilia, my wife, and protection not only for my physical identity but also for my spiritual identity, along with protection for my family. Indeed, I needed the family plan at this point in my life!

> We must continue to protect our homes and keep the enemy out.

I remember one day in my classroom getting into a dialogue with many of the students about relationships. I noticed a young lady sitting in the back of the classroom with a sad look on her face. I walked over to her and asked what was wrong. She asked me, "Mr. Lester, what do you do when you know someone who is really close to you who is cheating on someone else who is really close to you? What do you do?" Not knowing where she was going, I rebutted quickly, "If someone was cheating on you and your closest friend knew about it, wouldn't you want them to tell you?" The room became very silent for a moment, and then people started talking again. Taking all of what I said in, the young lady started to cry. "Thanks, Mr. Lester."

I immediately pulled her out of the classroom to find out what was wrong. She told me her dad was cheating on her mom and she knew about it. She felt something was missing because she didn't feel she could go to either one of her parents and talk to them about it. She felt as if her life and identity were being stolen from her. This girl was only fourteen years old. It is so important we protect our families from the enemy creeping in and stealing our children's identities and even our identities.

After I talked with this young lady for some time, she was able to bring her family together and listen to a speech I had given at a church, "What Our Youth Are Missing" (inspired by that young lady). She later told me that her whole family listened to it. Her dad confessed to her mom and things started to change for the better. I am glad God was able to use me in that situation so He could bring restoration to her home. We must continue to protect our homes and keep the enemy out because, just as Jesus says, a house divided against itself cannot stand (Matthew 12:25).

Pearl S. Buck reinforced this idea of a family plan: "The lack of emotional security of our American young people is due, I believe, to their isolation from the larger family unit. No two people—no mere father and mother—as I have often said, are enough to provide emotional security for a child. He needs to feel himself one in a world of kinfolk, persons of a variety in age and temperament, and yet allied to himself by an indissoluble bond which he cannot break if he could, for nature has welded him into it before he was born."

Paul Pearshall also spoke of the importance of alliance and protection of our family and family values: "Our most basic instinct is not for survival but for family. Most of us would give our own life for the survival of a family member, yet we lead our daily lives too often as if we take our families for granted."

III

TRUE-LIFE STORIES

We all know people affected by identity theft. Sometimes we are guilty of criticizing them for making foolish choices or behaving irrationally when really they are victims of the worst kind of deception, emotional overthrow, or bondage. We love many of these individuals dearly, wringing our hands and crying along with them when we should really function as spiritual agents (like the FBI) to get to the root of the matter.

I appreciate the honesty of these individuals (my friends) who eventually realized that they were victims of this spiritual predator. Here are their stories.

"Adversity introduces a man to himself."
-Author Unknown

CASE 1:

~

DREAMS BLOWN BY ILL WINDS

White dress, flowers, limousine, platinum rings—that's what every normal young girl dreams, right? I guess I wasn't normal then because, unlike my peers, I wasn't planning my wedding in high school. Actually, I thought marriage was for old people, so I didn't think that I would get married until I was in my thirties! Then I met Jeremy, the man who would change my life and ultimately be the basis for my testimony.

Jeremy and I had talked about marriage while we were dating, but he was in the military and I never thought I could be a military wife. However, I was in love with him; and when he received his orders to serve in Operation Iraqi Freedom, I realized that I wanted and needed to be his helpmate. After surviving the war, Jeremy was discharged from the military and we were married two months later.

Maybe the signs were there and I just didn't see them.

Two weeks after returning from our honeymoon, I was calling family, checking in with everyone to let them know we had made it back and how we were enjoying married life so far. Jeremy's cell phone rang while he was asleep. When I answered the phone, the soft voice responded, "I must have the wrong number." Then she hung up only to call again. "I apologize. I have dialed the wrong number again."

I said, "Maybe not. Who are you looking for?"

"Jeremy, but who is this?"

"This is his wife. Who is this?" I asked.

"This is his fiancée," she answered.

I wasn't ready for that one.

That phone call was one of many. They became redundant. I remember too well the list growing to at least five women. However, I stayed! What was I doing?

Maybe he was addicted to sex, so I started to accompany him to sexual addict meetings. It didn't work. Maybe it was posttraumatic stress disorder from the war, so I accompanied him to counseling. It didn't work. Well, not exactly. It worked for about a month at a time, before I found out about the next woman, then the next, then the next. Nevertheless, I stayed. Who was I becoming?

My self-esteem was so low that I let him be with other women and then come home to me. I remember him telling me once that he felt like he was cheating on one of the other women by being with me. But **I was his wife**! How could he make me feel like I was the mistress? What was I doing wrong? I felt worthless, as if I didn't deserve anything more. Apparently, Jeremy thought I deserved disrespect—and, boy, did he give it to me!

The physical abuse started after Woman Number Three. At first, it was slapping and pushing that later escalated to punching and choking. I vividly remember when Jeremy choked me while I was in the bathtub, looked me in the eye, and said, "I am going to kill you." At that point, he could have gone ahead and done so. I felt like dying anyway.

I went to the hospital twice because of the physical abuse. He also went to jail twice. I never pressed charges; I loved him. I even deserved it at times, right? Wow, the mind of an abuse victim is so damaged. What was wrong with me? Who in the world is this person I am looking at in the mirror? I used to be so strong (at least I thought so), now I'm weak and insecure. That didn't turn him on. It made him cheat and beat me more and more. I just wanted to die. I wished that he would just kill me. I didn't even recognize myself anymore.

Jeremy was on painkillers for an injury sustained in Iraq. I was on antidepressants, which seemed only to make me more depressed. I was done; I had had enough. His Vicodin was so appealing in our medicine cabinet, along with the Nyquil, Excedrin PM, and Sudafed. Jeremy was in the military and used it as an excuse for always having liquor around, so it was only natural for our cabinets to be filled with Jim Beam and rum. After all, I needed something to wash everything down.

I had thrown him out of the house for the eight-millionth time, and I was alone. I did it. I just took everything. I was so tired of living. I felt guilty about everything. I guess if I had really wanted to die, I wouldn't have called my mom to tell her what I had just done. She was in another state, but I knew she'd call Jeremy's mom and "mommy dearest-in-law" would show up. I blacked out so I don't remember her showing up, the paramedics, or the ride in the ambulance.

My attempted suicide resulted in my staying in a mental ward for a few days. Had I known that the suicide wouldn't work, I definitely wouldn't have wasted my time. Sitting in that ward was killing me in itself. What's worse, Jeremy never came to see me! What had I done?

I pleaded with my doctor to let me go after two days even though I was supposed to be in there a minimum of a week. I was so thankful. I had dealt with enough embarrassment at work with the bruises, the ruptured blood vessels in my eye, and the stitches to my forehead. I didn't want everyone at work to know that I had just hit rock bottom and tried to take my own life, too. I was released on Sunday and able to go back to work on Monday.

> The blood of Jesus covered me every time.

I'm here. I should have died that Friday night. However, I'm alive. I should have died from the blows of a man who was trained to kill people; yet, I'm alive. I should have died the night I was gasping for air in the bathtub when he choked me. Again, I'm alive. God is so merciful and forgiving. I shouldn't be here, but I am. I could have caught all kinds of STDs (sexually transmitted diseases), but I didn't. I could be dying from AIDS, but I'm not. The blood of Jesus covered me every time I was intimate with Jeremy, every time he laid his hands on me. Most importantly, His blood covered me when I tried to take my own life.

You may have noticed that this is the first time I have mentioned God or Jesus Christ. That's because it is true when people say, "You never know how much you need God until

He's all you got." It was when I hit rock bottom that I called out to God. I had nowhere else to go—but UP!

It didn't happen overnight. It was a process (it still is to this day). My identity was stolen. I'd look at my reflection and not even recognize the person I had become, but I knew that I didn't like her. First, I knew that I had to go back to the person that I was before Jeremy and then change her. You see, whoever I was at that point had some trait or characteristic that attracted people like him; so I had to make the pre-Jeremy image of me even better. I made it a point to reintroduce myself to the old me and compare and contrast her with the person I wanted to become.

Second, I had to surround myself with people who lifted me up. This meant subtracting people from my life and adding some new ones.

Third, in conjunction with that, I had to learn how to protect my heart. This didn't mean that I had to become ice cold, but I allowed God to grant me a discernment of those personalities and situations that tainted my existence. The Devil doesn't have any new tricks because the old ones still work! So the "new me" had to be able to distinguish between those who were contaminated and those who were healthy. Thank God for discernment! Now I was able to get my identity back and even allow God to transform me into someone even better. I was ready!

Now I desire and yearn for God. I now allow him to work on me, with no interruptions, so that I can continue to discover gifts, talents, and ideas within me. I am discovering something new about myself on a daily basis, and God is adding more to me each day. I recognize the person that He is molding within me. I love her more each day.

Jeremy and I are divorced now, but I'm no longer weeping over it. My marriage is dead, but I'm not. I chose me; I chose life. I don't regret anything. I thank God for Jeremy because I wouldn't be where I am today had he not been a part of my life. I wouldn't be a better me! I was able to grow in Christ because of my experience. I was able not only to find the old me but to be converted into a better me. I got my identity back and then some!

CASE 2:

~

DIMINISHED FAITH ALONG THE WAY

Never did I imagine that I would come to a point in my life where I entertained the thought of suicide. Not me! I'm in love with Christ and a faithful servant in the house of God every week. I paid tithes and had the fear of God in my heart. Then, all of a sudden, it was like my life hit a rock and my world shattered into pieces. First, it was my finances; I lost my job at the wrong time. I was engaged, trying to save money for a wedding. Everything was cool for a moment; then days became weeks, and weeks turned into months. Everywhere I inquired, the response was the same: "Sorry we're not hiring right now."

Four months went by and I had no job or steady income. The bills continued to accumulate. I fell behind on loans and credit cards. There were days when I wondered if I would eat or put gas in my car—$4.38 on Pump Number 8 or $2.12 for a double cheeseburger and a small order of French fries?

I found myself losing faith in God, and my fiancée began to lose faith in me. Because I had no steady income, I struggled to pay rent. I borrowed from Paul for the last time to pay Peter; now Paul had no more to give. Then the eviction notice came from the rental office with a thirty-day final warning. Where was my God? What did I do wrong? I felt worthless and ashamed. I didn't feel like a man. I couldn't provide for myself; how was I going to provide for a family? Should I rob? Should I start selling drugs? I thought about a lot of things I never thought about before. April 23, 2006, was the last straw that almost pushed me over the edge. This was my twenty-third birthday.

> The only thing that stopped me was God's grace.

My mother was in town for my birthday, and she was preparing a great meal for me and my fiancée. I went to the bathroom to wash my hands and I saw my fiancée's phone light up from a text message. Of course, I was curious so I picked it up. To my surprise, she was going back and forth with some guy, talking about me and how she couldn't wait to get away from me. Let's just say I read a whole bunch of stuff I didn't want to read. I called the guy from her phone, and he shared how they had met. Now they were beginning to be involved and all this crazy stuff.

This was **my** fiancée! I hung up in disbelief and went to confront her without telling her I had talked to the guy already. She told a boldface lie, repeatedly, until I told her I had talked to the guy and he had told me everything. My mother stood between us and jumped into the argument. She was angry that we were arguing over minute issues and decided to tell me for the first time that she had breast cancer.

I fell to the ground face first, as if I had been hit with a vicious left hook. I could barely breathe; I was in a state of shock. I wanted to choke the life out of my fiancée and embrace my mother at the same time as she stood there in tears. It was too much to swallow.

"Come on, I'm taking you home!" I yelled at my fiancée. I was furious! She stormed out the door, and so did I. I wanted to kick her in the back of the head! How could she do me like that? I thought she loved me. We got in the car and I screamed at her. She responded by screaming at me. We were both crying by now. I took off driving like a mad man, doing 80 mph in a 45 mph zone. I had no regard for the law, I could have cared less about traffic lights, and I didn't even care about my life at that moment. I wanted to take both of our lives that day. The only thing that stopped me was God's grace, of course, and the thoughts of my mother crying. Plus, my mother had already lost my brother in a car accident.

I didn't take my life that day, but I did I stop living for a little while. I stopped caring. No longer was I reading my Bible or spending intimate time with God. I traded my Bible study time for pornography. I began to watch it so much that I wanted to become sexually active again, so I began digging in my past, searching for old numbers. All the relationships and habits I let go to gain a new life in Christ, I picked up again. The girls that I once told I was abstaining from having sex were now in my bed—and we weren't just cuddling or watching movies. I became entangled deeper and deeper in a net. I had lost self-control. Church wasn't the same; the young man that once lifted holy hands and made a joyful noise unto the Lord was only going through the motions. I counted down the seconds for church to be over.

The same young man that used to be hungry to hear the word of truth now fell asleep in service. What was happening to me? Jesus and I were once tight, but I turned my back to gain pleasures of the world. I lost myself in my circumstances.

I'm thankful for grace and mercy! Eventually, I was restored to Christ and things started looking up for me; but for a while, I allowed the enemy to steal my identity. Once I looked away from the hills from where my help comes, I was an easy target.

CASE 3:

~

A TOUGH ROAD FOR A SINGLE DAD

I went through many changes during my senior year of high school and the next few years after high school. Many things I planned for my life did not take off as I had planned, so I began to drink and party.

I had had a dream of getting a football scholarship and playing professional ball since I was twelve or thirteen years old. I did extra things that other guys didn't do, such as getting up at 5:30 a.m. to run and lifting weights when others were playing around. My dreams of getting a scholarship dwindled away my senior year when I made the minimum score for the SAT late in the school year and when my high school coach refused to help me when colleges were asking for game film on me. I played for a man who gained my trust for most of my high school career and even received the Player of the Year award. However, he began to act like he didn't know me after my final season was over. I became depressed and started drinking for the first time.

I decided to move back to Chicago after high school and get a job. Although I liked Chicago because most of my family lived there, I decided to move back to Georgia to go to college after making a nice sum of money. I started going to Gordon College and realized that, a year and a half after I had graduated high school, the University of West Georgia was still interested in me playing football for them. My interests came alive again and I started working out and getting focused. I struggled the first year of college because I had a lack of direction and doubted if I was supposed to even be in college. I was discouraged and transferred to West Georgia as soon as I could. I had never considered playing football at West Georgia before, but I missed football and the feeling I received from the crowd when I made a big hit. The coach at West Georgia stated that he could only give me a partial scholarship because I transferred late but he would have more money for me the following year.

My Christian walk was compromised because of women and partying, but I wanted to do well and live the way my parents raised me. I repented and tried to stay on track despite the fact I had doubts about Christianity. College professors and even my older brother would reference places in the Bible that were inconsistent and plant negative seeds. My first year at West Georgia was tough.

I was arrested with three other teammates for shoplifting during the summer practice season. I was not discouraged and worked my way up from eighth string linebacker to third string when my coach decided to move me to defensive end. Despite breaking my wrist and hurting my back, I managed to maintain confidence. During spring football practice, I moved from seventh string defensive end to first string. My coach did not offer additional scholarship money despite my accomplishment. I quit the team but returned when my defensive end coach got me more money. That aggravated my head coach, but I didn't know it. The fall season of my second year, I dislocated my shoulder and lost my starting position because I missed two practices due to injury. My head coach did not allow me to start again even though I outperformed other defensive ends on the field.

My grades began to drop and I began to struggle with depression as I had in times past, even wanting to commit suicide. I never wanted to be alone, so I was always finding new women or spending time with my friends and smoking weed. I had received multiple injuries in football and was not getting along with my head coach.

I quit the football team when one of the women I was sleeping with told me she was pregnant. I thought she was ruining my life because she wasn't my girlfriend and I didn't trust her. I had only been with her for two weeks. I didn't trust anybody, especially women, because my last girlfriend cheated on me when I went home for the summer. The women in college always said they couldn't trust me because I had a sneaky smile; so, out of frustration, I lived up to their expectations.

> I knew I needed God because . . . my life was out of control.

I confronted the woman I made pregnant, who happened to already be the single mom of a four-year-old boy. I told her it would be better if she got an abortion because we didn't have anything going on. I told her if she kept the baby that I would take care of the baby but couldn't make a commitment to her. She wouldn't take no for an answer and continued to try to manipulate me, but I wouldn't budge. I finally agreed to take care of her through much drama, but she had the abortion anyway because I refused to commit to her.

After she had the abortion, I began to feel guilty and wanted to make things right. Eventually, we ended up together again. This time I developed a soul tie. I could not get away if I tried.

She dogged me out for the way I treated her the first time she was pregnant, but I took it and just wanted to make things right. I ended up getting a job and moving in with her. I stopped spending time with my friends and focused most of my time on her. We had a very emotional relationship because of the abortion, and I prayed that God would give us another baby just like the one we had lost. She became pregnant again. I even knew the very night it happened. This time I said I would do things right. A month before she was pregnant, I bought her a ring and was determined to take care of her.

At this point, I knew I needed God because I felt like my life was out of control. I was addicted to smoking weed despite getting bad weed that made me deathly sick. It affected my lungs and was laced with a substance that made me hallucinate.

I used to repent and ask God to help me make it through the night so I could straighten out my life, but I continued to make the same mistakes. I finally rededicated my life to God; I got saved. I was excited. My girlfriend made the same commitment to God, and we decided to stay together.

I began to get revelation that I never had before. I began to get closer to God and my life started to change. I stopped smoking, drinking, and hanging out with thugs and some of my friends. I became convicted of shacking; but every time I tried to leave, my fiancée had a fit. We decided to get married before she had the baby.

I was now working two jobs and was back in school determined to get my degree and make life better for all of us. I also continued to get closer to God, but my wife didn't. It did not bother her if she went to church or not. She told me that I was losing my edge and that she liked me better when I was more thuggish. I continued to work odd jobs, making sure my family was well taken care of; but my wife didn't seem to appreciate me. She always brought up the fact that she had aborted a baby and that God hadn't forgotten it. Every time we had an argument, she would bring up the abortion; but I had patience and lived with it.

During our first year of marriage, I began to realize that she didn't love me and, no matter what I did, did not appreciate me. She constantly made remarks to hurt me and even said that she was disappointed with our child because she thought that she would end up light skinned with good hair like her momma. My wife also decided to check out mentally. By the time the baby was six months old, I found myself taking care of my daughter the majority of the time even though I worked full time and was still in school.

For the next three years, I found myself with either my stepson and my daughter or my daughter most of the time. My wife opposed everything I did, but I finally graduated and landed a better paying job in a factory. My wife worked against me and I felt like I had to fight the world all day and then go home to deal with a wife who was bitter. I constantly prayed for my wife and one morning at about 3:00 a.m., God asked me if I would rather lose my wife for her to be saved or hold on to her. I told God that I was willing to let her go.

A year later, after getting a big promotion on her job, my wife left me and filed for divorce. She left my daughter with me and took off. She tried to come back a few weeks later and trick me to get my daughter, but she did not prevail. I pleaded with my ex-wife not to take me to court because I heard from God and He told me to try to settle it outside of court. However, she wouldn't listen. She was shocked when we appeared in court and saw that I had my facts together and that the judge was going to see proof that I took care of my daughter twenty-four days out of the month. Then, she was ready to settle out of court.

> I just wish that more parents, especially men, knew that children are a blessing from God.

My ex-wife and I ended up getting joint custody, which meant that my daughter would be with me every other week and that she would be with her mother every other week. The arrangement did not bother me because I had taken care of my daughter since she was six months old anyway.

I made a commitment to treat my daughter like a princess and show her what a godly man looks like so that, when she is old enough, she will make better choices than her parents. I would say that raising a daughter is a challenge (especially when her hair needs to be combed), but I appreciate the time I have been able to impart into my daughter's life. I just wish that more parents, especially men, knew that children are a blessing from God.

CASE 4:

~

WHEN CURSES STALK YOUR BLOODLINE

Do we really know how our identities can be taken away so easily? God has a purpose and a plan for all of our lives, but I believe we allow Satan to interfere. I once read that we have three voices in our lives: God's voice, Satan's voice, and our own. God is going to quietly say what He has to say and keep it moving. He will not try to out shout the other two voices. It's up to us to make the decision to listen up and hear what He has to say and carry out His orders. However, because Satan's voices continue to argue with one another so strongly, we end up doing what we think is right for us to.

Generational curses also have a lot to do with not knowing who we really are. A lot of people get caught up in becoming who their parents and other family members are. My mother and grandmother were alcoholics, and my favorite aunt who I love dearly was gay. My stepfather was not a man by God's or my standards at all.

We never had stability in our household. As a little girl, I remember moving a lot. I also remember not having daily full-course meals and being home alone a lot. Needless to say, my grandmother—who later became my inspiration—always tried to keep the family together. Unfortunately, she was very uneducated when it came to teaching me the lessons of being a

> God has a purpose and a plan for all of our lives.

young woman and becoming a mature adult. No one taught me financial planning, the importance of remaining a virgin, or even thinking about and planning my future. I was always instructed to finish and graduate high school, as if that was supposed to be the end of my educational experience and going to college didn't matter after that.

Mentally, I thought it stopped there. Backtracking my story, even though I suffered in so many ways, I was always blessed. My aunt made sure I was involved in extracurricular activities and school events. She also made sure I spent quality time with my family. As I became a teenager, of course, my hormones were changing and I felt I needed a boyfriend. Again, no one ever explained to me or taught me how it should be when it came to having a relationship with the opposite sex.

Needless to say, I stayed single to the end of my eleventh grade year. During my senior year, I fell in love with a fellow classmate who, in the beginning, did not give me the time of day. However, I was so determined to get him to like me I literally forced him to like me in return. Even though I thought it was love back then, looking on it now, I know it was not. Once we crossed that line of just being normal teens that liked each other and had sex, I was mentally gone in my head. I had truly lost my God-given mind. I felt that he was all I needed to make my life complete. At this point, I was very young and uneducated about life and how a young woman should go about living hers; and soon after, we started dating or going together, which was the common term used back then.

A while after we had been dating, I ended up getting pregnant. By then my boyfriend had already signed up to join the army. Of course, I had no clue how to raise a child; nor was I ready financially. I started to look for jobs and apply for trade schools. I ended up going to school to become a medical assistant and working at the same time.

Throughout my pregnancy, I still did not know what I was getting myself into. I knew I was in love and hoped to eventually marry my boyfriend and have his baby so we could all be one big happy family.

As time passed, we stayed together and I ended up having three more children. I was in a very messy situation. Not only did I have three more mouths to feed and clothe, but I was also alone in Maryland. My boyfriend was stationed in North Carolina. He was able to live his life as freely as he wanted.

Imagine being alone and having four children, three of them that are very close in age: three, one, and four months. I would cry sometimes not knowing what I was going to do. I ended up putting my life on hold to raise my children. After all the fights and bouts of deception, I married my high school love—something I would later learn wasn't the right decision for either of us at the time. We were not ready for marriage and all the other issues it would bring.

The first year was great, and then the relationship went downhill from there. I know that sounds familiar since so many people say the same thing about their marriage experience, but that's really how it was. While we were married, I had discovered that during his stay in North Carolina he had fathered another son.

Through our ten years of marriage, there were good times and bad times. Our struggles had to do with not knowing each other's true identity before we were married. We were both still dealing with generational curses. I battled with him and my stand on Christianity. I felt that, if my children and I went to church, my husband should come with us. If he didn't attend, then I felt like we shouldn't go without him. I also struggled with how to be a mother as opposed to a friend to my children. A lot of decisions I made were not decisions that a mature mother would have made.

Then my husband and I decided to separate. We later divorced. My kids were not mentally or emotionally ready for that change in their lives; and to this day, they have struggled tremendously, mostly my oldest three. I have dealt with behavioral changes, poor performance in school, and family altercations. Through all of my troubles, one thing I can say is God has always been there for me and continued to look out for my family, even when I wasn't obedient to His word.

Life is full of lessons. Although I'm a lot older and more mature, and thankfully wiser, I realize I will always continue to learn until I leave this earth. Those lessons learned already have begun to help me discover my identity that was masked so long ago. I will continue to be thankful for that. Ten years of my life were stolen because my identity was not intact.

IV

SAFEGUARD ALERT: PROTECTION FEATURES

A number of pitfalls contribute to identity theft. Some of them stare us right in the face. Others are not as easily noticed. It is so easy to miss the signals and fall into behavior patterns or form associations that open the door to the spiritual robbery of our souls' purpose. However, we must watch carefully for certain telltale signs along the road that signal caution. Watch out for protection features.

PROTECTION FROM DIS-TRACK-TIONS

~

"A person who aims at nothing is sure to hit it."
-Unknown

Have you ever felt like you've been on a specific path and something has made the effort to dis-track you from getting to your destination? Whether it was a job, the children, the phone, negative people, family issues, or problems in general, somehow you felt as though something had pulled you away from where you should be.

Let's say, for example, we are on a track about to run a race. Let's also suppose that the finish line is destiny or wherever God has ordained us to go during our lifetimes. Suppose the team we're up against is known for cheating and making their opponents lose by rigging the track. This example is symbolic of life; the enemy wants to dis-track us, to cheat us or to stop the drive in us to complete God's race. The Bible says, "The thief does not come except to steal, and to kill and to destroy; I have come that they may have life, and that they may have it more abundantly." John 10:10 (NKJV)

> Whatever it is you dream to become or pursue, you must . . . block out all of the unnecessary things to become who God created you to become.

Dis-track is made up of the prefix *dis-* which literally means "to deprive of" and the root word *track*, which means "a course laid out or a path."

Therefore, *dis-track* means to "deprive of a path."

It is so easy to get out of focus when we allow something to enter our lives that has no importance or significance in being there. I remember watching the Olympics several years ago and seeing the sport of archery. I was fascinated by how the archers could hit targets hundreds of yards away with bows and arrows. Repeatedly, I saw archer after archer take a stand, aim at the target, and strike it to gain several points. After thinking about it, I truly believe the archers' focus and training enabled them to hit the target from a considerable distance. Although the archers had thousands (if not millions) of people watching, I believe they knew that the target they wanted to reach was more important.

Likewise, we can learn from the sport of archery. When God gives us a specific target—no matter who is watching or what circumstances may arise—we are to stay focused so we can hit the target we are aiming for.

It would be a very funny thing to watch the sport of archery only to see archers shoot their bows and arrows and hit something other than the targets. Whenever we allow *dis-track-tion* to enter our lives, the target we are designed to hit becomes clouded and out of focus. The very fact that you're reading this book is because, like the archer, I am aiming to hit the target of your heart.

If I don't take the time to focus, my purpose and destiny will be stolen by the dis-track-tions of the enemy. Whatever it is you dream to become or pursue, you must make sure you block out all of the unnecessary things to become who God created you to become. We have too many people missing the mark because they are shooting at targets that will not produce anything in their lives.

What are you shooting for? Are you focusing or allowing circumstances to steal your true identity? What have you done today to ensure you hit the target and arrive at the destination God has for you?

We must also remember that shooting at the wrong target is the same as doing what the enemy wants us to do—nothing!

I have discovered three ways to persevere in the midst of dis-track-ions:

1. **Keep your eyes on the target.** We must always keep what we are going to do in front of us. The moment you take your eyes off the right target, you will focus on the wrong target or on no target at all. It is senseless to allow not focusing to stop you from becoming all that God has for you.

2. **Know that there will be dis-track-tions used to try to stop us**. We must maintain a "whatever-it-takes mindset": No matter what it takes, we must press towards the mark. Paul the apostle constantly reminded us that his main goal was to press onward despite what he was going through. In the book of Philippians, which he wrote while in prison, he penned these words: [12]"Not that I have already attained, or am already perfected; but I press on, that I may lay hold of that for which Christ Jesus has also laid hold for me.

¹³Brethren, I do not count myself to have apprehended; but one thing I do, forgetting those things which are behind and reaching forward to those things which are ahead, ¹⁴I press toward the goal [or target] for the prize of the upward call of God in Christ Jesus" (Philippians 3:12-14 NKJV).

3. **Trust God.** We must trust God even though we cannot see Him and sometimes cannot feel Him. The more we lean on Him, the stronger we become. It is very natural not to believe what we cannot see, but we must understand that faith sees what the natural cannot see. Our faith will be the very thing that will honor and please God. The worst thing we can do is pull away from God when we have gotten off track and don't know how to get back on track. In Proverbs 3:5-6, we are encouraged to trust God with everything at all times.

Remember, distractions will stop anyone who pays close attention to them.

> The more we lean on Him, the stronger we become.

PROTECTION AGAINST YOUR PAST

~

"When we marry our past, we divorce our future."
-Terence B. Lester

What you need to know about the past is that, no matter what happened, it all worked together to bring you to this very moment. This is the moment you can choose to make everything new—**right now**! It is amazing that we see our futures through old lenses, outdated and useless for seeing what the future holds. It is utterly amazing how much our pasts can corrupt or create our identities and futures. Our experiences from the past can help us to avoid the wrong things in the future and give us the proper wisdom to handle different circumstances. I once heard a speaker tell his large audience, "Only bring the past with you if you are going to build from it."

However, if you intend to build from your past, you must first heal from your past and let go of those things that have become baggage weighing you down. What have you allowed to weigh you down from your past? What are you holding onto that has you only giving half effort? It is extremely important to make a decision to let go of your past if it is contaminating your identity in your present. I have been healed and learned from a collection of all of the past events that were hurtful to me, which has enabled me to write and speak as I travel today.

I remember a hot Wednesday afternoon when Jerry, a friend, and I were strategizing on how to make our dreams reality. His words remain with me to this day. He said that one of the greatest gifts a person can receive from God is deliverance from the opinions of other people and their pasts. He is slightly older and a lot wiser than me; so whenever I need advice, I sit and listen to him speak from experience. I asked why he felt this was so important. He stated that some of us grew up or associated with people who have such strongholds on our minds that our decision-making is predicated on what we believe they will think about the moves we are contemplating. He said that our past hurts hold us back from moving forward if we do not learn how to let go.

When he told me that, I imagined traveling to the destiny that was marked out for me with thousands of bags, only to find out those bags were things I had held onto for years. It is a great misfortune to try to become what God wants you to become while traveling with unnecessary baggage. Destin Figuier informed us, "The past can't see you, but the future is listening."

I realized that Jerry was right. So many people never move beyond where they are because they allow their pasts to dictate every move. As a result, our identities and purposes are stolen. Negative thoughts and reminders of our pasts could have us thinking that we are not making any progress.

> If you intend to build from your past, you must first heal from your past.

Here are three questions that will allow you to know if you are still holding on to your past.

1. **Do you think about it more than your think about your future?** Some people never move forward because they only think about what they have gone through, not where they are going. In the Bible, Israel sinned and turned away from God several times. However, God never looked at their past; He always saw a bright future for His people. In Jeremiah 29:11 (NKJV) this is what God says to His people through his prophet: "For I know the thoughts that I think toward you, says the LORD, thoughts of peace and not of evil, to give you a future and a hope." We must understand that God never gets so angry that He does not want to give us a brand-new start. If you are thinking about what you have done or what you have gone through, it is now time to drop it and move forward. God has something entirely better.

2. **Are you stuck?** One of the greatest tactics from the enemy is to put us in a place where we are so stagnated by our pasts that we become stuck and have no strength to move forward. The past can contaminate us to the point our confidence flees and the enemy can have his way because we stop pursuing new things. He wants our courage to leak out so that we become discouraged from moving ahead. It is detrimental to live one day over and over in our minds when we can never actually relive it again. Yet, we may have gone weeks, months, or years feeling as if our lives are stuck in our pasts. I encourage you to take your identity back by pressing on to something new, something that will

affect you and your future totally. Move past this stuck position and regain your confidence and identity.

3. **Is your past affecting those close to you in your present?** The worst thing is to allow our pasts to haunt our family relationships, partnerships, and home environments. Most of the time, problems that weigh us down affect those closest to us the same way. Not only are we weighed down, but those who love us the most are also hurting. This produces negative environments. The only way to renew our environments is to start fresh and refrain from speaking those particular things in the atmosphere. It has been said several times that our words create our world. Change your word usage and change your atmosphere.

The first step to getting over your negative past is to forgive yourself. Choose to forgive yourself and your past. Create a brand-new future by replacing your old picture of your life with a better picture of your life.

PROTECTION AGAINST UNFORGIVINGNESS

~

"Unforgivingness cages the soul of a man or woman."
-Terence B. Lester

Unforgivingness steals our identities, and the person(s) God wants us to become. When we make bad mistakes in our lives or are the victims of wrongdoing, we can be tempted to hold ourselves responsible or to carry grudges against other people. When we do this, we inflict punishment and condemnation upon ourselves. We do harm to our own identities. Granted, we may have been partially or totally responsible for what happened; but that doesn't mean we have to condemn ourselves for the rest of our lives. Joseph F. Newton observed, "People are lonely because they build walls instead of bridges." Some people will live one day over and over, hating themselves forever and never acknowledging that God has freed and forgiven them for what they have done or what others have done to them.

That's why I love God so much: His love sets us totally free. I know this is a well-known scripture, but John 3:16-17 (NKJV) says, "[16]For God so loved the world that he gave His only begotten Son, that whoever believes in Him should not perish but have everlasting life, [17]For God did not send His Son into the world to condemn the world, but that the world through Him might be saved." His sending His son says that He forgives us.

> Unforgivingness . . . will cage you like a prisoner; and the only way to release yourself from that cage is to use the key of forgiveness.

Jesus took on everyone's problems and sin and died so we may have that freedom and relationship with God once again. The problem we have is forgiving ourselves and those around us. It is not a good thing to go through life having been forgiven by God but acting as if we're not. I like what Catherine Ponder said: "When you hold resentment toward another, you [are] bound to that person or condition by an emotional link that is stronger than steel. Forgiveness is the only way to dissolve that link and get free." Whether the unforgivingness is toward yourself, someone else, or a situation, it will cage you like a prisoner; and the only way to release yourself from that cage is to use the key of forgiveness. Forgiving ourselves will set us free.

Unforgivingness, even when aimed at oneself, can linger long enough to do considerable damage to our identities and life goals. Unforgivingness is manifested in several forms:

- Resentment
- Pride
- Grudges
- Jealousy or envy
- Anger or rage

In addition, unforgivingness can plant a root of bitterness that can result in the following:

- Closed doors to spiritual growth
- Physical illness
- Increased worry
- Emotional imprisonment of the person who refuses to let go
- Destruction of the vessel that harbors it

In an effort to be totally free of unforgivingness, I wrote a letter to certain people in my life to express my feelings so that I could finally be free and move forward. You may wish to use it as a model for your own letter or to form your own communication.

Lewis B. Smedes said, "You will know that forgiveness has begun when you recall those who hurt you and feel the power to wish them well." Once I shoved unforgivingness out of my life, I was ready to focus on a whole new world with a new perspective. I could not move forward without it.

Dear Loved One,

Today you are receiving this letter in sincere appreciation of your relationship to my life. Recently, I have had a life-changing experience. As my life has progressed and unfolded, I have had to overcome many obstacles, all of which have made me the person that I am today. Although I have grown to be a good person, I believe God has taken me through several testing and training periods to show me the final area from which He wants me to be set free.

The reason I'm writing this is that as we become transparent before those who love us, God is able to heal us and free us. I can honestly say that I've overcome a lot of my past, but one thing that I haven't overcome to this point is unforgivingness.

Unforgivingness has been the root of my anger and unhealed wounds. This has kept me bound. God has convicted my heart as I've never felt before. He simply said, "Let unforgivingness go or you'll be stuck at only that level of growth." I really want to grow and be all I can be for God; but I understand that, with each level that He takes us to, we will not be able to get there without shedding unfit baggage or learning what He is trying to teach us.

I want to be the best speaker and writer He has created me to be, and I don't want anything to hinder Him from unleashing an anointing. I want you to know if I have ever caused you any pain or made you feel as though you couldn't get through to me or as if I wasn't cooperating, it was not your fault at all. It was the unforgivingness within me and the unforgivingness and anger that I hold on to when someone does me wrong.

As you read this, I declare that I am free from unforgivingness. I also understand that I am totally nothing without God and the valuable relationship that He has given me with you. A great man once said, "A friend is an extension of self." I want you to know that you are an extension of me. I love you and appreciate you, and I sincerely apologize.

I understand that God is really trying to draw greatness and potential from me, and I won't stunt my growth because I will not be able to move to the next level until I pass this test.

The rest of this year, I will be happy that I'm alive and learn further how to forgive, let go totally, and put it in God's hands. I truly and sincerely accept the things that I cannot control. I truly have a grateful heart and want to be the best that I can be.

Unforgivingness is like a prison filled with poison, bondage, and chains that hold us back from going on to freedom and future blessings. From this day forward, I am a different person.

I love you and want you to know that I have let my anger and unforgivingness go!

Love,
Terence

PROTECTION AGAINST LACK OF FOCUS

~

"Concentration is the secret of strength."
-Ralph Waldo Emerson

Once we have forgiven our pasts, we become strong enough to focus on our futures. Remember the earlier example of a race and the reminder that we move in the direction upon which we focus. When we start to focus on where we are going instead of where we have come from, even the things that we have gone through teach us valuable lessons we can then teach to others. We can work on ourselves and zero in on the destinations God has for us.

I want to share with you a story I read in a chain email. I really never read forwarded messages because they all seem cheesy and routine. However, this one caught my attention as I started to delete it. It is called "Blurred Vision":

> *A businessman was highly critical of his competitor's storefront windows. "Why, they are the dirtiest windows in town," he claimed. Fellow business people grew tired of the man's continual criticism and nitpicking comments about the windows. One day over coffee, the businessman carried the subject just too far. Before leaving, a fellow store owner suggested the man get his own windows washed. He followed the advice. The next day at coffee, he exclaimed, "I can't believe it. As soon as I*

washed my windows, my competitor must have cleaned his too. You should see them shine."

It is so amazing how focusing on someone else's flaws, shortcomings, and idiosyncrasies can steal identity. It stops us from working on ourselves. All too often, we are so worried about what we have gone through or what others have done to us we are unable to grow and work on self. It is very easy to point the finger, blame, and lose focus on self-growth. Confucius once declared, "Don't complain about the snow on your neighbor's roof when your own doorstep is unclean." Jesus Christ encouraged us within His Sermon on the Mount to focus on self and not judge others. He was simply saying we cannot grow self with focus that is distorted.

I fell in love with this quote by Elsie Kerns, a well-known author: "Our wounds become our gifts." She was right in many ways. It wasn't until I forgave my past and started to focus on my purpose (identity) that I discovered how even my past was designed by God to equip me to do the very thing that I'm doing today. When I started to focus on helping others in the areas from which I was healed, I found my true purpose for living.

> It is very easy to point the finger, blame, and lose focus on self-growth.

If you are driving a car, it is necessary to look in the direction you'd like to travel. Even if you want to go in reverse, there is a rear view mirror to allow you to see where you are going.

Wouldn't it be crazy to want to go in reverse in a car while looking forward? That's why we move in the direction we look.

If we are living in the past instead of going forward with our lives, we can possibly be in the process of falling further and further behind. To move ahead from our pasts, we have to change our focus. We must set our minds on things that are greater than our pasts so our identities won't be stolen because of misdirected focus. After we are in focus and looking in the right direction, we must then get rid of anything else that stands in the way of building and protecting the identities that will move us forward. We must also eliminate excuses: "shoulda, woulda, coulda," and so forth.

Here are three things to help you stay focused:

1. **Remind yourself constantly why you are doing what you are doing.** It is so easy to lose focus when we forget why we are doing something. I understand that by finishing this book while I'm going through chaos myself I'm doing this for God and you. God wants you to know you are special to Him, and it is on my heart to let you know how He feels. If I were to stop because of how I'm feeling, you would never read any of these words. Whatever you're doing right now, you must remind yourself how great the end will be once you reach your destination and accomplish the very thing God wants you to accomplish.

2. **Develop a consistent spirit.** Most people lose focus because right after they remind themselves of the

reasons they are doing something, they lack the consistency to keep moving forward. It is easy to do something one day, two days, a week, or even a couple of months and then stop; but the people who stay committed regardless of whether they see change or not succeed. God will use your consistency to promote your growth to become all that He has for you.

3. **Build a good support system.** Many people lose focus because they lack good, solid support. We can do nothing alone, but we can do everything with togetherness. It was the wisest man in the Bible, Solomon, who declared in Ecclesiastes 4:9-12 (NIV), "[9] Two are better than one, because they have a good return for their work: [10] If one falls down, his friend can help him up. But pity the man who falls and has no one to help him up! [11] Also, if two lie down together, they will keep warm. But how can one keep warm alone? [12] Though one may be overpowered, two can defend themselves. A cord of three strands is not quickly broken." He was saying we cannot go through life without support. The right people around you will help you stay focused. The wrong people will distract you and help you lose focus. You choose!

To strengthen our focus, we must find targets worth shooting and shoot at them with consistency. We must understand that the level of consistency we have in our lives determines the level of focus we possess.

PROTECTION AGAINST NAÏVETÉ

~

"Stop a moment, cease your work, and look around you."
-Thomas Carlyle

Being naïve is one of the greatest threats to identity. It opens doors for counterfeit objects and circumstances to be misinterpreted as real or authentic. Naïveté creates a sense of numbness wherein we can't feel what's real anymore. It accepts dysfunction as functional.

> Often we become involved in situations that produce so much pain we accept them as functional. We become naïve.

I'll never forget running into an old friend in the mall. I hadn't seen this young lady since we left high school. "Hey, Terence, how have you been?" she said.

"I've been well." I answered with a big smile.

"Why are you smiling so hard?" she asked,

"I'm happy to be alive," I replied. I then told her about all the wonderful things God had done for me in my life. I told her I had become involved in ministry, written several books, married, and recently had a beautiful little girl. She responded with less enthusiasm.

"I wish I could say everyone is doing that good," she said.

"What do you mean?" I was genuinely concerned.

She then told me about one of the young ladies we knew who had also gone to school with us. "She is in this relationship with this guy and the situation is really bad." I asked her to explain. "Well, he is cheating on her, he doesn't do anything to contribute to their child, and on top of all that, he hits and beats her. She has had to call the police on him several times and even has been to the hospital for domestic violence. I have told her time and time again to cut it off, but she keeps saying she is going to stay there because she believes he is going to change."

Knowing a young lady who had lost her life to domestic violence, I felt a cold chill run down my spine. "Why do we do things that aren't good for us until it kills us?" I asked.

In the ensuing silence, as we just stood there for a few moments, I became even more upset that our old classmate was going through this at the age of twenty-three. Naïveté was stealing this young lady's identity. Sometimes we become so numb to dysfunction that we are made weak and don't even know it. She was naïve to stay with the hurt and the pain.

My former schoolmate then told me the young lady called her almost every day. "She is always crying her eyes out because of some new madness," she said.

I shook my head, my heart heavy with concern. "I will pray for her and that God gives you the wisdom to be there for her and help her get out of that dysfunctional relationship." She agreed and then we parted ways.

When I left the mall, the only thing I could think about was why this young lady was staying in a dysfunctional situation and not leaving. Immediately, I heard the word clear as day: **naïve!**

Often we become involved in situations that produce so much pain we accept them as functional. We become naïve. We become accustomed to dysfunctional behavior, and it becomes a part of us. It numbs who we are as people and eventually steals our identities. We become so blinded by pain and naïveté that we waste so much time. We become so comfortable in being in a mess that we no longer have a desire to fix what's broken. Has being naïve stolen your identity? Are you in a situation that's causing you much pain but you refuse to let it go because you define who you are by the pain you feel?

The answers to these three questions may be red flags to let us know we are being naïve:

1. **Do you accept constant hurt as a way of life?** The lady my former schoolmate and I conversed about accepted hurt as a way of life. We have to learn how to cut off those things that produce nothing but bitterness and pain.

2. **Do you know the right thing to do but ignore it?** The young lady knew the right thing to do but didn't act upon that knowledge and common sense. She had parents, friends, and even doctors tell her the truth; but she refused to do the right thing because she had become accustomed to the pain. You need to do the

right thing even if it means going against how you feel. If not, you may suffer even more destruction.

3. **Do you carry these two into every situation?** When most people overcome these things, they forget the lessons and take the same problems into different situations, becoming naïve all over again. Once we come out of these situations, we must learn the lessons well so we don't repeat earlier mistakes.

In the Bible, God's chosen people rebelled against Him many times despite everything He did for them. They kept being naïve and worshipping other gods that couldn't do anything for them. The only thing God wanted from His people was to be loved and to be the object of their worship. When His people didn't show proper respect, He allowed them to go through things to teach them lessons. He allowed their enemies to take them captive several times. He did not allow their captivity so their enemies could rule forever, but He wanted to teach them something. He wanted them to lean on Him when all else was failing. He wanted them to be wise because He was wise, not naïve. God's Word boldly declares, "My people are destroyed for a lack of knowledge. Hosea 4:6 (NKJV)" Sometimes being naïve too long can cause us to miss our purpose and waste time. It even causes the enemy to rob us of who we are. It can literally rob us of our identities without us knowing it.

I believe each of us is similar to a bank account. We have the capacity to be deposited into and we have the potential to be withdrawn from. When we are deposited into, it is because we have placed ourselves in positions to receive things that have added to us, not subtracted from us. We have placed ourselves in positions to be multiplied, not divided. We have put ourselves in positions to hear from God, not from dysfunction. Dysfunctional behavior causes us to be diminished every time.

The things that withdraw from us are usually the things in which we have invested our time and energy without receiving positive returns. *Withdrawal* means something is being taken out to go somewhere else. If it is not going to a place that will allow you to grow, it isn't good. How many times are we naïve and are withdrawn from? How much time do we waste because we don't do our homework?

I don't know what happened to the young lady, but my prayer is that being naïve did not cost her, her life. We should never allow being accustomed to dysfunctional behavior steal that which God has created us to be.

PROTECTION AGAINST COMPROMISE

~

"There are only two options regarding commitment. You're either in or out. There's no such thing as a life in-between."
-Pat Riley

One of the easiest things in the world to do is compromise. People are involved in some form of compromise on a daily basis: some for good reasons, others for bad. Although compromise can go either way, I want to look at how compromise can literally distort who we are. If not controlled properly, compromise can negate or work against identity.

Some time ago, things weren't going well for me financially. I had been in my marriage close to a year, and I was enrolled in Bible college. I was pursuing my bachelor degree in theology. I felt that, after God allowed me to turn my life around and accomplish many great things, He was calling me into ministry. When I started school, I only had half of the tuition I needed. It was the last paycheck I had received after being laid off. However, there was something within me directing me to pursue what God was calling me to do.

Not having money to pay my tuition at times was difficult. I questioned why God called me to do something that I had seemingly little power to accomplish on my own. There were times when tuition was due and then overdue. I remember going to the school almost a year without making a payment. I had been there close to two and a half years. Things were tight for me. I was in a place where I was powerless. I wanted to complete the assignment God had for me; but at the same time, I felt I couldn't because of the lack of resources.

All of this time, I felt the pressure of being married, pursuing ministry (a field that doesn't guarantee a great financial return), and trying to keep my faith at a level to keep me from compromising and going back to my old ways.

I waged war with compromise: staying faithful versus giving in to those things around me because I was weak. All the while I went through this emotional turmoil, it seemed that every friend who wasn't pursuing a righteous path had everything I didn't. They were prospering while I was suffering. I saw people living the good life, but I also saw they had no relationship with God.

Would I succumb to what those around me were doing because I wasn't experiencing what seemed like perks at that particular time? Should I quit? Those were the questions I was asking myself. I came to the point where I felt everything I was striving for was not coming to pass.

> Compromise is an awful predator that steals our identities when we are weak.

What have you strived so hard to bring into manifestation that has not come to pass? Are you at the end of your rope or ready to quit? Are you about to compromise what you see so clearly during a moment of weakness? No matter how weak we become, we must not compromise because the cards seem to be stacked against us. We must never compromise because we feel everything we have done has been in vain.

In my situation, compromise involved going back to my old ways and personality. Sometimes when we give out so much and get nothing in return, we begin to ask, "Why am I even doing this?" Once we question our purpose, the identities into which God is trying to make us, we revert or we abort the process. Compromise is an awful predator that steals our identities when we are weak. Whenever we are going through tough times, we must not compromise to do things we have long left behind. If we do, we create a revolving door of conformity.

During my last semester in school, I had to pay nearly ten thousand dollars before I could receive my degree. Otherwise, all of the classes I had taken would have been in vain. I felt weak at times, as though the mountain of debt was too big for me to conquer alone. At those times, I heard a still, small voice encouraging me to stay faithful, not to give up or give in to any sort of compromise.

Through my staying faithful, God provided payments for the tuition. He did it in such abundance that I had a credit of $2.32 that the school returned. I graduated with my bachelor degree in theology.

During the course of this trial and subsequent victory, God show me four things we must never do when compromise presents itself:

1. **We should never take matters into our own hands**. When we choose to do so and the matter is too big for us to handle, we quit and compromise

what we are trying to accomplish. There must always be room for God to work in our lives.

2. **We should never count God out**. Many times, God will hold things from us until the right time. I call this "faith training." He builds our faith to see how much we will trust Him. I once heard a man say, "Delay is not denial."

3. **We must never give up**. Compromise is nothing but giving up before the reward. We must never count our dreams out because it is taking a little bit more time than we anticipated. I once read this quote from an anonymous author: "If you can find a path that doesn't have opposition, then it probably doesn't lead anywhere." We must understand that sometimes receiving things of great value means overcoming certain opposition.

4. **Never lose self-worth**. We must not define who we are by what we are going through. If we lose our self-worth, we lose our esteem to stay faithful to what God is doing in our lives. Many people compromise their identities because they elect to forfeit their self-worth.

More than anything, the Devil wants you to lower your standards while you are waiting on a breakthrough, promise, or dream. I'm reminded of Jesus in the wilderness. The Devil tried so hard to get him to compromise His standards. He tried to use the discomfort and inconvenience of the wilderness to make Jesus forget all that He came to earth to accomplish.

However, Jesus, well aware of His Kingdom authority and mission, refused to lower His standards. He recognized the harassment as temporary hardship (Matthew 4:1-11 NKJV).

If you are at the end of your rope, I challenge you to tie a knot and **hold on**. Never compromise what you stand for. Don't give up on your purpose for living. Don't give up on the passion you once felt. Don't let your standards drop because of adversity. I encourage you to look adversity in the face and say, "I'll never compromise because I know who I am."

PROTECTION AGAINST EXCUSES

~

"Excuses nail you to an average life filled with failure and limitations."
-Terence B. Lester

Excuses cause people to lose their innate desire to grow and become something better. The next stage in getting over your past is to eliminate excuses.

Many well-known people began their lives with difficult childhoods, but they eliminated all their excuses to get ahead. They didn't let the bitter things of life destroy who they were destined to become. Likewise, we must not allow our past to grant us permission to create excuses. I admire the reflections of Francois De La Rochefoucauld, a noted French author: "Nothing is impossible; there are ways that lead to everything, and if we had sufficient will, we should always have sufficient means."

> Excuses . . . prevent us from succeeding and developing our true identities.

If we are not careful, excuses can rob and steal our identities. Benjamin Franklin said, "He that is good for making excuses is seldom good for anything else." It has also been said repeatedly, "Excuses give us permission to stay where we are." You'd be surprised at the number of individuals who simply quit trying because they think they are too short, too tall, not funny enough, or not smart enough. We must not let our excuses hinder us from making progress. I love the old saying, "It doesn't matter how we start; it only matters how we finish." I want to add one more conditional truth to that, "if we eliminate our excuses!"

Excuses allow us to cancel our responsibilities for self. They say to self, "Live life without boundaries," which wrecks our identities. Responsibility tells us we are responsible not for what we have but for what we can have, not for what we are but for what we can become.

Excuses are harmful because they prevent us from succeeding and developing our true identities. The moment we make excuses, our constant answer to life's challenges and problems, excuses start to become our natural beliefs. Our beliefs ultimately become the very things that shape and mold us into to who we become. Our beliefs become self-fulfilling prophecy. The Bible tells us several times that we shall have what we say; and most naturally, we usually say what we believe. Once we accept responsibility and eliminate all the excuses we give, we free ourselves so that God can work on who He wants us to become. We must evaluate our actions and take corrective measures, God-given solutions, to our problems. As one great speaker said, "Excuses become like stop signs; they halt our progress."

I believe they also halt the continual development of our identities.

When we refuse to make excuses and embrace self-responsibility, God allows us to reap many rewards. Many wonderful things are brought to us because of this attitude. It floods our lives with self-respect, selfless pride, encouragement, promise, and confidence. Therefore, we must understand that making excuses can put the brakes on our progress, while accepting responsibility can lead us to where God wants us.

These three principles will aid us as we plan to stop making excuses and start building better identities:

1. **Always take responsibility.** We can never move forward or progress unless we have chosen to take ownership of who we are and where we are. Once we take full ownership, excuses then begin to vanish like mist in the air. By accepting responsibility, we give God open doors to develop us and reconstruct our identities. We must resolve to accept responsibility today—right now. As one man once told me, "Don't find an excuse, find a way. Don't make excuses, make good." Remember what Winston Churchill said: "Responsibility is the price of greatness."

2. **Examine your progress weekly, monthly, or yearly.** Everything has measurements. You probably got up this morning and made a cup of coffee, fixed a bowl of cereal, or bought your favorite breakfast sandwich from a restaurant you visit often. Everything we like, own, and consume is made to specific measurements. We too must take the time to evaluate our progress. Many people give up on themselves because they never acknowledge the growth they have made.

Whether it is reaching a month on a diet, reading a book for a week, or refraining from saying certain words, we must affirm that we have made progress.

Examining self simply builds confidence and consistency. People who never stop to check the oil in their motors eventually blow the head gaskets, leaving them broken down on the road to purpose. Compare where you are now with where you would like to be. Ask yourself why there is a gap between these two points. Then chart a plan to get there. Don't make excuses. Make plans and take corrective actions.

3. **When you drop the ball or mess up, learn from it and do not repeat it.** A great man once said, "Use your time for discovering solutions instead of inventing excuses." We must not let excuses creep back into our systems because we have failed or dropped the ball along the way. That is why self-evaluation is critical. It helps us stay focused, keeping our minds on the main thing. There is treasure in every trash. Some of us think we will never recover from the trash of life. Then there are those who see differently, those who decide to recycle and make something again. If you fail, you must learn to continue without excuses.

For us to tap fully into everything we are to become, we must take away every excuse. By doing so, we tear down the barriers we've placed on ourselves. A wise man once told me, "We are the only creatures on the face of this planet that has the power to use our minds against ourselves." What a true statement! When we use excuses, we use our minds against ourselves by not taking responsibility. We must eliminate excuses and become who we are destined to become.

> Our beliefs ultimately become the very things that shape and mold us into to who we become.

PROTECTION AGAINST DEVALUATION

~

"In order to feel valuable, you must love yourself."
-Terence B. Lester

If you use a national shipping service, you may be asked to declare the value of the items being shipped. Usually, there is a limit on the liability (dollar amount) the shipper will assume. If you are traveling from one country to another, customs officials may require you to declare certain purchases or items bought during your travel. It then becomes necessary to list the items and their cost (value). Just as retail goods have a market value, you also have human value. It is up to you to declare your total value and, believe me, to God you are precious—more so than precious **gold**!

Strange things happen to us when we don't know our value. We set ourselves up to be undervalued and misused. To begin to imagine our value, we should search the Word of God for confirmation. No one on earth knows us well enough to determine our true value. God is the only Ruler of the earth and Assessor of merit. He alone can measure our value.

Three unfortunate things occur when we question our value:

1. We become discouraged.

2. Our faith begins to decline.

3. We begin to imitate what feels comfortable (people).

I will never forget a life-altering remark a wise man of God made to me a long time ago: "Terence, you're a mighty man of valor. You will be great and stand before nations!"

Mighty? I said to myself, not thinking very highly of myself at the time. Valor? Me? Nations? Why? I thought. At that moment, I neither looked mighty nor felt mighty. I didn't even know what valor meant. I just figured that valor meant something excellent because he was smiling when he said it! As a great man of God once said, "Before you invest, investigate." I needed to examine exactly what he was calling me **before** I chose to believe it.

I searched the Scriptures for the word *valor* and found this illustration: When Gideon was faced with what appeared to be a task too great for him to achieve, "the Angel of LORD appeared to him and said, 'The LORD is with you, mighty man of valor.'" (Judges 6:12 NKJV)

Before the word from the Lord came to Gideon, he had no idea of his value. On many occasions, he, like us, believed that he had to fight the battle with what he could see in the natural (circumstances). Like Gideon, we have to be reminded of the value of the Lord's army (people) and the value of His investment in us. Whatever the battle, if we try to fight in our own strength, we'll lose every time. Just because we cannot see God does not mean He is not there with us. Just because we can't hear God, doesn't mean He is not there listening to our prayers. Just because we cannot smell God, doesn't mean that He isn't there, ever knowing. God is omnipresent: **He is everywhere at the same time**! Jesus has given us His guarantee: "Lo, I will be with you always"(Matthew 28:20

NKJV). We should never forget the value of our Almighty Companion! Remember that "true value is found inside out, not outside in."

> To God you are precious—more so than precious **gold**!

PROTECTION FROM OBSTACLES

~

"Obstacles cannot crush me. Every obstacle yields to stern resolve. He who is fixed to a star does not change his mind."
-Leonard DaVinci

If we are not careful, the obstacles of life have the power to steal who we are. When I think of not allowing problems to get the best of us, the story of Helen Keller comes to mind. At nineteen months old, she became blind and deaf due to what doctors called a medical condition originating in the stomach that affected some of the senses controlled by the brain. In spite of great odds, Helen Keller overcame her disabilities and became a world-renowned author and speaker. Today, she is remembered as an advocate for people with disabilities and for numerous other causes.

Keller didn't allow her problems to steal the purpose for which God created her. She wrote, "When one door of happiness closes, another opens; but often we look so long at the closed door that we do not see the one which has been opened for us."

> You must always view yourself as an overcomer.

I couldn't agree more. We should not allow our problems to blind us from seeing opportunities. As I said earlier, I love this quote from Frank A. Clark: "If you can find a path with no obstacles, it probably doesn't lead anywhere." Many individuals have overcome problems and, in spite of them all, have later become who they were destined to be.

One of my most favorite stories in the Bible begins in Genesis 37 and continues until Genesis 50, the last chapter of the book. It is the story of a young man named Joseph. Joseph was one of the last sons born to a man name Israel (Jacob). Joseph grew up with plenty siblings (brothers). He had both his parents in the house, but there was one problem. One day, God gave Joseph a dream of what he would become and accomplish with his life. Out of sheer joy, Joseph told his father and all his brothers. Thinking they would support him, he shared his heart. To his surprise, his brothers hated him for the dream; and his father gave him no support. Imagine God giving you a dream and, out of excitement, sharing it with those who you feel have your best interests and finding out they hate you? They don't think much of you? They could care less for you? How would you feel if your own family overlooked you? After he shared this news with them, his brothers put him in a ditch and later sold him into slavery. What type of family support is that when you share your ideas? The one thing I love about this story is that little did Joseph know he was put in that situation to save his family.

He never complained the whole time his family mistreated him. He never said, "I'm going to get even." He never said, "I'm going to hold a grudge." He never even said, "I hate God for putting me in this situation." The whole time he was in slavery, and even when he went to jail, the Bible says that God caused Joseph to prosper everywhere he went. Why? I believe it was because Joseph chose to focus on God and on building his character. When Joseph received that dream, he was a teenager. When it finally came to pass after all the mistreatment, he was thirty years old. God used Joseph to help Pharaoh save the land they lived in because of the famine that had come. Joseph's family and his brothers were saved, too.

In essence, although Joseph was overlooked, he never allowed his being overlooked make him feel left out. You may be in a family in which you feel misused, neglected, or taken for granted; but you have to understand you are not left out. God still has great things He wants to do through you that will ultimately benefit you, your community, and your family. Although we can't choose the families we are born into, we can choose to help change our families for God. That starts by changing ourselves.

Although simple, I have found three practical things Joseph did to maintain his sanity and ultimately reach the destiny God had for him.

1. **He respected those who disrespected him**. There are times you will have to show respect to people who are not concerned with your best interests. You may feel doing so is causing them to win at their own game, but it's not. It's helping you release the extra baggage you can so easily accumulate. It helps you stay strong. I once heard a man say, "Whatever angers you, controls you." That's a very true statement. Have you ever been upset at something and that was all you could think about through your whole day? Nothing feels the same. It throws your whole day off. Well, that's what the

speaker meant. Whatever upsets you, if not dealt with, can throw off your days, months, and even years. That's why Joseph still maintained his respect for his family and his brothers, not for them but for himself. Something magical happens when you uphold your character in the face of negative kinfolk. It makes you a better individual and, ultimately, builds who you are, your character and self-worth.

2. **He held onto to his dream**. There will be times when some family members will say so many awful things that they will have you thinking that what God has placed in your heart is way off the mark. Joseph's own brothers tried to make him feel as though what God said couldn't happen. Who in your family has told you, you weren't smart enough, tall enough, or prepared enough; that you couldn't make it; that you couldn't start that business, organization, or ministry; or that you couldn't raise your children by yourself and still go to school? Who in your family has opposed the very thing God is trying to create in your life?

Joseph could have given up on those dreams because his family overlooked his potential. He could have thrown them away with his self-esteem. But he didn't. He held onto the dream God had given him. In the pit, he held on to it. In jail, he held on to it. When he was lied about, he held onto it. What are you in right now that's causing you to forsake what God has said? Whatever it is, drop it and hold onto your dream.

3. **He never complained or got mad at God.** In Genesis 50:20 (NKJV), Joseph says, "But as for you, you meant evil against me; but God meant it for good, in order to bring it about as it is this day, to save many people alive." Joseph let his brothers know that everything God had taken him through was meant for good. He chose not to complain.

When we feel wronged, the most natural thing to do is to complain, to throw pity parties and to invite the magnificent guest Me, Myself, and I. We do this so we can feel better about feeling worse. However, doing so really makes us feel the worst. Through everything that happened, Joseph never complained. Our situations are usually much better, yet we still get mad at God because we don't understand why these things happen.

The thing I love most about this story is that Joseph chose to work on himself and not his family. In the end, when he reunited with his family, he stood before them and declared that what they meant for evil, God meant for good. Can you see the good God is working even when you don't understand it? If not, it's probably because you've let complaining and anger blind you.

Personally, I always felt I was an outcast in my family; and certain things confirmed it. No, I don't hate my family; and yes, I do love them dearly. But there were times when I felt I just didn't fit. Sometimes family members know how to make you feel as if you aren't worth anything. Is that you? If so, I want you to know you matter. You matter to God and you matter to me. You have so much to fulfill in this life, but the way to do it is to follow the example of Joseph and continue to work on self. Make yourself the best person you can be. Despite everything you are going through, you will make it. A great speaker once said, "When you're walking through Hell, keep walking because you'll make it out."

How do you view yourself? Most of the time, the way we see ourselves is the way we respond to life. You must always view yourself as an overcomer to overcome your problems. If there appears to be no knock on the door of opportunity or, worse, no door on which to knock, there is strength within you to build your own door and knock on it yourself!

Life is like mathematics, and God is like the answer key. When life gives us problems, God has the answers to solve them. Helen Keller understood that she was an overcomer despite her odds: "We can do anything we want to if we stick to it long enough." This blind, deaf woman overcame great odds to encourage others to do the same. I believe that her life is a testament to what we can do if we don't complain!

PROTECTION FROM COMPLAINTS

~

"If you don't like something change it.
If you can't change it, change your attitude.
Don't complain."

-*Maya Angelou*

Complaining not only steals our potential but weakens our faith and destroys our hope. It literally steals who we are. Anytime we complain, we delay our ability to build anything worthwhile on the inside. Complaining affects not only us but also our surroundings and viewpoints. People generally complain when their patience is running thin or when problems overwhelm them to the point that they take it out on everyone or everything around them. I believe complaining is the Number One killer of spirits and joy.

Complaining is evidence of unbelief. I love this passage taken from "Complaining Only Makes Things Worse," written by Dr. Dale A. Robbins:

> *Regardless of whatever circumstances may cause discontent or dissatisfaction, complaining is always an expression of unbelief toward God's order in our life. You see, the whole premise of Christianity is that Jesus becomes the Lord (boss) of our life and our circumstances. They are in his hands. Thus, if believers complain, it really becomes an accusation against our Lord, in whom we've*

trusted our lives. "for the LORD hears your complaints which you make against Him. And what are we? Your complaints are not against us but against the LORD" (Exodus 16:8). (See also Psalm. 106:24-26)

Complaining is unbelief in God's Word which says, "all things work together for good to those who love God, to those who are the called according to His purpose" (Romans 8:28). If the Christian really believes that the Lord is in control of their life, and is working "ALL THINGS together for our good," he will stop complaining and start thanking the Lord for the plan He is working together for us.

Even when the Devil comes against our faith with trials that are "not so good," God will even turn these situations around and "work them together for good" as we remain steadfast in faith. Don't become bitter and start complaining, but continue to praise God and give thanks to God "in spite" of all things. This will prevent the Devil from overcoming you with discouragement and will send him fleeing. "In everything give thanks; for this is the will of God in Christ Jesus for you" (1 Thessalonians 5:18).

Thanksgiving is the expression of gratefulness and faith in God and is the very opposite of complaining. Giving of thanks expresses appreciation for what God has done, what He has promised, and the confidence that He is directing our life with His order and provision. God will answer prayers and work on the behalf of the thankful (Psalm. 50:14-15).

Complaining leads to excuses and excuses lead to putting things off. In "The College Blue Book," Anthony J. D'Angelo wrote, "If you have time to whine and complain about something then you have the time to do something about it." I agree with him because complaining not only wastes time but also has no effect on what we want to see changed. The only way to beat complaining is by weeding out the negative thoughts. When negative thoughts come, we always have to be aware that there is a bright side. Sometimes when our thoughts go flat, we just have to pump them back up so we can get rolling again. When we complain about the small things, we scare away the big things destined for our lives. Complaining also causes us to use what I called curse words in my book *U-Turn*. Have you cursed lately? Well, maybe you did and did not know that you were cursing left and right, all day long! And, no, I'm not talking about the expletives that we all know too well. I'm talking about talking down to yourself.

> Complaining is the number one killer of spirits and joy.

PROTECTION FROM CURSE WORDS

"You have to expect things of yourself before you can do them."

- Michael Jordan

Many times, we use curse words without actually using profanity. A true curse word is a word that leaves our mouths and diminishes the power to achieve. It also positions and empowers an invisible brick in front of us every time we use one of these words. Some people use these words so often that the bricks eventually build a wall, and they hide themselves behind their curse words. Someone once said that cursing is a poor excuse for an underdeveloped vocabulary.

Maybe you have been cursing and just don't know it. Here are the curse words you should look out for and the things you should say to replace them, antidotes or vaccines that fight toxic substances.

The Curse	**The Antidote**
I can't	I can.
I don't believe	I am a true believer.
I'm not worthy	I am worthy.
I quit	I'll work harder.
I give up	I will never give up.
I'll try	I will accomplish.
I wish	I will have.

I'm not good enough	I am the best I can be.
I don't know anything	I will learn what I don't know.
I'm a loser	I'm a winner by faith.
I want that	I will own that.
I can never see myself	I can see myself reaching anything I envision.

I broke the habit of cursing myself by simply thinking positively. Positive thoughts kill negative words. We must use positive words to solve our problems; otherwise, problems will steal our identities. Therefore, we must remember that curse words are the words we use against ourselves and our own abilities. Don't allow your problems to steal your identity. Protect yourself against your problems!

I love "You Tell on Yourself," a poem by an unknown author. This attention-grabbing poem gives us further insight telling on ourselves by the way we live and what we speak.

You Tell on Yourself

You tell on yourself by the

friends you seek,

By the very manner in which you

speak.

By the way you employ your leisure time,
By the use you make of the dollar and dime.
You tell on yourself by the things you wear,
By the spirit in which you, your burdens bear.
By the kind of things that make you laugh,
By the records you play on your phonograph.
You tell on yourself by the way you walk,
By the things of which you delight to talk.
By the manner in which you bear defeat,
By so simple a thing as how you eat.
By the books you choose from the well-filled shelf,
In these ways and more, you tell on yourself.

So there is not a particle of sense,

In an effort to keep up a false pretense!

To stop cursing yourself, you must take time to encourage yourself, invest in yourself, and most importantly **believe** in yourself. Most of our dreams are stolen by the words and negative thoughts that come out of us. The Bible declares in Proverbs 18:21 (NKJV), "Death and life are in the power of the tongue, and those who love it shall eat its fruit." The very thing you speak to yourself most will produce tangible evidence of what you believe. Stop cursing yourself and start speaking life.

> A true curse word . . . diminishes the power to achieve.

PROTECTION AGAINST PROCRASTINATION

~

"Someday is not a day of the week."
-Author Unknown

Procrastination is another negative tool that impedes our accomplishing goals and hinders us from walking our purpose. As I stated earlier, I had many reasons not to finish this book. I had my past haunting me and other problems slowing my progress; but even with all of that going on in my life, I could not let preoccupation with adversity steal my personal identity. I remember sharing the idea of this book with my wife and later speaking on this topic at a church youth day. I outlined several factors that the enemy uses to steal our identities.

As the months passed, I realized how important it was for everyone to obtain this information. Sometimes we don't move ahead because we become comfortable. Historically, comfortable people want to stay right where they are. Have you been in bed on a cold windy morning, knowing that it was time to get up but being so comfortable that you just wanted to lie there?

I could not afford to procrastinate. It is an enemy to progress!

Not too long after I spoke on this subject, it was as though the very words that I taught started to oppose me. More problems came. Whenever we are faced with difficulties, the natural thing to do is—nothing! Sometimes we talk about what we

> **Procrastination is nothing more than a comfortable thought that holds no action.**

want to do but then never get around to doing it. I remember an entire series of negative events right after speaking on that subject. My wife and I experienced great financial hardship, some of my high school classmates lost their lives, and my grandmother was diagnosed with breast cancer and had to have surgery.

The thought of speaking about what I wanted to teach while in the midst of all those troubles was the hardest thing for me. I knew what I was created to do; but at times, I did not feel I could do it because of the circumstances around me. After all, just like you, I am much more human than I am divine!

Often I felt myself procrastinating in regards to operating in my purpose. Negative thoughts arose to discourage me: "You can't do it. You shouldn't even go through with it." That's why I loved it when I read the words of Eva Young: "To think too long about doing a thing often becomes its undoing."

After you protect yourself from your past and from problems, you must protect yourself next from procrastination. Even after we guard ourselves from the previous thieves, we still have to choose to move forward, pressing to live our purpose. I've found that procrastination only enters our minds when we give excuses to feel comfortable. When I say comfortable, I mean being locked into a comfort zone so that we don't want to move forward and take a risk! Procrastination alone can hold us back. Procrastination is nothing more than a comfortable thought that holds no action!

All thoughts are the foundation of action, and all action involves thinking. Thinking can do either of two things: either encourage you or discourage you! The thought of encouragement can push you to achieve goals; the thought of comfort can cause you to procrastinate or feel at ease. Feeling too at ease doesn't produce much! We are made to endure **pain** to **gain**!

I remember praying to God for the strength to continue pursuing the things He had charged me to do. All I could hear in my spirit was, "Keep going, My son." As I told you before, I mentioned to my wife and one of my closest friends the idea of this book. From the time I prayed, even till now, literally everywhere I encountered signs about identity theft and protecting yourself from criminals: signs and billboards, commercials on the radio, and so forth. Each time I saw those signs, I procrastinated about writing this book to address the matter from a spiritual standpoint until the final blow came.

I was sitting in my office, asking God in prayer what He was trying to say. Why am I going through so much? Why hasn't my material moved as You desire? These words settled in my spirit: "I'm trying to show you who you are in Me. I want to show you how much strength you have in Me."

That's what I believe He is trying to show each of us: that after He has healed us from our pasts and given us peace in the midst of storms, we have to activate the faith we've obtained through action. That's when I decided the best way to get something done is to begin. Anything short of getting started is simply—procrastination! I also want you to understand, however, that even after we act, there is no guarantee that things will happen right away.

What have you wanted to start or finish? I encourage you to keep going! There is such a thing as appearing to have life when actually there is little evidence to support the claim. I remember writing this devotional in my newsletter:

Life Support

*This morning, as I was getting ready for work, these two words popped into my mind, **life support**. For a moment, I thought to myself, "Where in the world did those words come from?" but after pondering for a while, I understood why my spirit had that powerful feeling about those words.*

Today we live in a "just enough" society. Let me clarify. Average has become the norm. Most people live to do just enough to get by; just enough to say, "I have a dream," yet fail to work it diligently; just enough to say, "I tried," and not enough to say, "I've given my all." Recently, I've been working on a project that I want to give birth to real soon. No, I'm not pregnant. I simply want to bring life to the dream that I've been given by God. I've been working on this project for almost a year now, *and it has taken me through a lot of bends and curves, ups and downs, highs and lows; but through it all, I have not given up. Although lately I have been slacking just a little on it! When I heard these words **life support**, they hit close to home because I believe God is saying to all of us, "Son, daughter, child, **stop** living your life on life support. Do more than just enough to get by!"*

Life support in the hospital is an incredible mechanism that sustains life and temporarily replaces the function of vital organs. Just the mention of these words is enough to send family and loved ones into deep despair. Many times, it signals the very end of someone's life.

Is there anything in your life that takes the place of your real abilities? What are you using as life support?

1. People

2. Friends

3. Work

4. Family problems

5. Personal problems

6. Success

7. Possessions

What are you using to live a "just enough" life? What is it that replaces normal (God-ordained) function; that if taken from you, you do not really exist? I believe that we all should fully disconnect from trust in things and people and hook up all of our trust in God Almighty. He is faithful to give us an abundant life, unconditional love, protection, peace, and safety.

Have I given up on this particular dream? Absolutely not! I'm working even harder to give life to what God has given me! I understand there must be adequate groundwork before the building! I would like to leave you with this scripture from the Bible:

Jeremiah 29:11(NIV) "For I know the plans I have for you," declares the LORD, "plans to prosper you and not to harm you, plans to give you hope and a future."

A Lesson on Life's Highway: There Is a Reason!

The simple things in life often deliver tremendous life lessons. Another piece I wrote, "Roadwork," relates to us reaching our full potentials and walking our purpose.

Roadwork

Some friends and I were on the interstate highway one Saturday when we encountered some extremely heavy traffic. It was so heavy that we were at a complete standstill. Whenever I'm in traffic, I have unbelievable patience. I heard cars honking and people cursing and witnessed all other types of agitated behavior. We sat in that car and didn't move for at least thirty minutes before we started to creep slowly forward. Normally, when there's a lot of traffic, it's because of rush hour or a car accident. In this case, it was a Saturday; however, the traffic was still amazingly heavy. Normally, on weekends, traffic moves much faster.

On the expressways, there are large signs overhead that indicate exactly what's going on; but we couldn't see one yet. Everyone in the car took a guess at what was slowing the traffic down. One of my friends thought it was an accident, the other thought that it was just busy, and I thought that maybe they were working on the road. As the traffic began to pick up, we finally saw the monitor. It read as big as day, "ROADWORK, EXPECT DELAYS."

We got to our destination, yet my thoughts were still focused on the big words on the monitor that said ROADWORK. I started analyzing why it is that every time people are working on the road, there's slow movement in traffic. After thinking for at least an hour, my spirit spoke to me and said, "Terence, if you are going anywhere in life, you will have to do ROADWORK"; meaning, if we're walking a path to destiny, before we get to destiny, we'll have to put in work to get to that destination.

ROADWORK is the actual training and sweat that we encounter while riding on less-than-smooth concrete. Initially, all concrete is rough and has to be worked to become a smooth surface. In life, there are going to be rough spots and bumps; but as long as we're putting in sufficient roadwork, we have nothing to worry about. The Bible says, "All faith without works is dead" (James 2:26 NKJV).

Roadwork: Taking the Time to Work Your Path

Sometimes people panic when roadwork has to be done and things are delayed. We do not get angry at the wait; we get angry at the work that has to be done that causes us to wait. We are required to put in work on the roads we are traveling in life. There are going to be times when things seem to be going very slowly, but it's simply because there's work in progress. If we are diligent on the road to success, we'll build foundations that are concrete, solid. I know what if feels like to sit on the highway of life; but as long as we are focused, we will see our destinations. We may not get where we want to go immediately, but we will arrive when the work on our roads is complete.

PROTECTION AGAINST SELF-SERVING PHILOSOPHY,

MISUSE OF POWER, AND POSITION

"Character makes a person who they are, not position, power, or level of philosophy."
-Terence B. Lester

Never confuse education with who you are. Throughout my life, I've had the privilege of meeting some very influential people with high status, power, and position. Some of those people were the gentlest and most respectful people I've ever met. Some had attitudes like mean rattlesnakes. However, by meeting those people, I learned several things concerning education and philosophy and how they can literally rob or steal our identities.

When I looked up the word *philosophy* in Webster's dictionary, I was intrigued by its definitions: "a: pursuit of wisdom; b: a search for a general understanding of values and reality by chiefly speculative rather than observational means; c: an analysis of the grounds of and concepts expressing fundamental beliefs; d: the most basic beliefs, concepts, and attitudes of an individual or group." I was excited when I saw that education and philosophy were the pursuit of wisdom.

I remember my return to high school to graduate after I had dropped out. I refused to get a G.E.D and chose to re-enroll to finish. My classmates were all excited about the different schools and colleges that had accepted them and the different scholarships they were receiving for full rides academically. I was a little confused as to what college I wanted to attend. Heck, I didn't even know what I wanted to do with my life because I'd just barely made it out of high school. Eventually, I selected a technical school because I never thought I would attend college. After one quarter, I decided to attend a regular college.

While searching to find my purpose, I found friends in different colleges with similar stories. Most of the individuals I encountered throughout my college career told me that they were in college because their parents expected them to be. Some even were majoring in the fields their parents had chosen for them.

In reflection, I think of all the college students in school who are going from major to major trying to find their purpose in life as I was. I've even run into people with whom I graduated who had the GPAs to get into the colleges of their choice and get scholarships as well. They are now working in fields in which they have little interest or feel almost no fulfillment. I ask myself, "What is the value of education if you are pursing it in opposition to your purpose?" If we were to take a poll on how many people are unhappy in the field in which they work and for which they have degrees, I believe the majority would say they are unhappy. Why?

> You don't have to have a college degree to serve.

If you are operating outside your original design, identity, or purpose, nothing will fill the void in your life. I admire what Dr. Martin Luther King, Jr. said: "Success, recognition, and conformity are the bywords of the modern world where everyone seems to crave the anesthetizing security of being identified with the majority."

Some of those people who have made it to high positions are there because that is where they are supposed to be. Others have assumed roles of leadership only to boost their egos and tickle their arrogance. I told you earlier that I've met people in high positions who have mean attitudes and who are bossy; they think because they have a certain level of education or status that they have arrived and that everyone is to respect who they are.

Horace Greeley, an American journalist and educator, stated, "Fame is a vapor, popularity an accident, riches take wing, and only character endures." I also heard a great orator state that if you want to test a man's character, give him power.

If we are not careful, the positions that education or philosophy make available to us could literally steal our characters and identities. We are all supposed to use our positions, status, and power to become beacon lights for mankind. Dr. Martin Luther King, Jr. also said, "The function of education is to teach one to think intensively and to think critically . . . Intelligence plus character—that is the goal of true education."

I believe that is a true statement. We should not only obtain an education to seek financial goals, material possession, and popularity but to make sure that we do not lose focus of helping others learn to think while empowering them. Walker Percy stated, "You can get all A's and still flunk life."

We do not have to be in the highest positions or have the most toys to realize that, when we are operating in our purpose wherever we are, we are to serve one another. I believe that's why Dr. King stated, "Everybody can be great because anybody can serve." You don't have to have a college degree to serve; neither do you have to have subject-verb agreement in all sentences. You only need a heart full of compassion. You need a soul powered through love. When we have the wrong attitudes concerning success, we begin to abuse others.

Whenever I went to work at the warehouse, one of the jobs I held previously, I'd do the very best that I could. Even though I often performed far beyond expected on tasks, my manager treated me as if I was nothing more than hired help. When customers came in to buy materials, he allowed them to talk to me any kind of way. I was in school at the time, working toward my degree and that was about the only job I could qualify for. The manager knew this and thought I was only working there. He had no idea that I was a twenty-two-year old young man in school and about to be married, a writer and speaker working hard to achieve my purpose. He saw me only in the light that his perception allowed. Therefore, he bragged on his position, power, and degrees. I never complained or disrespected him. I only kept the picture that I was striving to become on the inside. My pastor, Bishop Dale Bronner, once said, "The picture that stays in your mind becomes real in time."

Some people allow their success to rob and steal their real identities. I encourage you that, if you are in a high position, you devote equal energy to becoming a person identified by great attitude. The better our attitudes as leaders, the more people will want to follow.

Genuine leadership is the keenest asset in leading and motivating people. A leader is like a compass and has the capacity to lead others in the right direction, whether north, south, east, or west. Leadership is motivation with the right action. Too many people allow their level of power to steal their purposes for being in leadership positions. You must not allow power, or even lack of power, to steal your purpose for being in a certain place.

Many adults, teenagers, and children allow the wrong people and the wrong things to lead them. This causes them to gain little ground. You must find someone who contributes significantly to getting you where you want to be in life if presently you don't have the right models in your home, work, or school.

I like to read books of leaders who understand what it takes to overcome and live lives of purpose. You can't be a leader without first following someone who has covered similar ground and soared to a place you want to be. A great professional ball player would never be great if he didn't have a coach (leader). He would never make it to the professional level without the desire. He would never be inspired without the encouragement of the team.

> A leader is like a compass and has the capacity to lead others in the right direction.

You need people to invest in you: a team of good friends or mentors. Leadership is born from a chain reaction. Every great person has followed a great person, and everybody is capable of being great—if each chooses to follow. In the past, I thought a person could lead people with aggression and control; but I found that aggression spoils the spirit and control rattles the mind. That's why we must stay protected against our pasts because past hurts cause anger.

Remember, to get ahead in life, you must have three things in place:

- The right leadership
- The right desire
- The right encouragement.

You can only lead the way you have followed and been taught. In prayer, one thing I always ask for is guidance because without it, we can't give it. I've found that as long as you follow the best, you will lead the best.

If we are not careful, our success and achievement or alignment with certain philosophies can go to our heads. We should remain humble and keep the main thing, the main thing.

Jesus taught in the New Testament that those who are greatest will be servant of all. (Matthew 23:11 NIV) He was clearly stating that leaders and people with power should give, and set an example for those who follow them.

The Giving Leader

One of the greatest forces in the universe is a simple act of kindness. Great or small, we can all display this quality in life. This story I heard a motivational speaker tell illustrates a simple life lesson.

Paid in Full

One day, a poor boy was selling newspapers door-to-door to pay his way through school. He was homeless at the time, had little money, and was very hungry. He decided he would ask for a meal at the next house. However, he lost his nerve when a lovely young woman opened the door.

Instead of a meal, he asked for a drink of water. She thought he looked hungry and so she brought him a large glass of milk. He drank it slowly and then asked, "How much do I owe you?"

*"You don't owe me anything," she replied. **"Mother always taught us never to accept pay for an act of kindness."***

He said, "Then, I thank you from my heart."

As Tim Baker left that house, he not only felt stronger physically, but his faith in God was strengthened as well. He had been ready to give up and quit.

Years later, that young woman became critically ill. The local doctors were baffled with her illness. They finally sent her to the big city, where they called in specialists to discuss the rare disease.

Dr. Tim Baker was called in for the consultation. When he heard the name of the town she came from, he went down the hall of the hospital to her room. Dressed in his doctor's gown, he went in to see her. He recognized her at once. He went back to the consultation room determined to do his best to save her life. It just so happened that when he was struggling in school, he studied how to treat her rare disease. He was going to give up school, until God spoke through the nice young lady. From that day, he gave special attention to the case. After a long struggle, the battle was won. Dr. Baker requested the business office to pass the final medical bill to him for approval.

He looked at it and then wrote something on the edge. The bill was then sent to her room. She was afraid to open it, for she was sure it would take the rest of her life to pay for it all. Finally, she looked, and something caught her attention on the side of the bill. She read these words: **"PAID IN FULL WITH ONE GLASS OF MILK"**

(Signed) Dr. Tim Baker

> *Tears of joy flooded her eyes as her happy heart expressed gratitude, "Thank You, God, for telling me to plant seeds into people, even when I didn't see a field in my own life."*

No matter how much you know or where you are in life, if you give anything, give with **sincerity** and **kindness**. You'll never know who is on the other side of the gift in the future. Light matches, but don't burn bridges.

A close partner to kindness is the nature of one's attitude. Did you know that our attitudes greatly determine how we live our lives? Our attitudes greatly affect our emotions and are the fires burning behind our visions in life. For instance, if our attitudes are negative, our thoughts are most likely going to be negative. When we leave people, the thing they remember most about us is our attitude. Earlier I discussed individuals who had realized tremendous success yet had attitudes that made other people feel uncomfortable. They seemed to enjoy watching other people squirm. Attitudes are one of the most powerful weapons we possess. We have full authority over our attitudes.

To control our attitudes, we must control our thoughts. A motivational speaker once said, "It's not what happens to us, it's how we let it affect us." Our attitudes determine our outlook on the world, and our outlook on the world reveals the world in us. We must never allow the education we have obtained, the success we have had, and the knowledge we have gained boost our egos and steal our identities and purposes for living. We must serve as Jesus informed us. We must remember that positive attitudes can change the world around us.

> We have full authority over our attitudes.

PROTECTION AGAINST WRONG ASSOCIATIONS

"Books, like friends, should be few and well chosen."
-Rainer Maria Rilke

If we are not careful, the wrong relationships can leave our lives in turmoil and lead us down the wrong paths. More importantly, the wrong relationships can steal our identities. I've encountered numerous relationships that I'd been better off without. I am sure that you too have had relationships that held you back or failed you, relationships that changed you, and relationships that saved you.

Relationships that held you back in many ways were due to the incompatibility of those relationships. Maybe you were headed down one path and your friend or companion was headed down a different path. Maybe your focus was on a different level. It doesn't mean that either of you were bad people; it's just that the relationship was not the relationship that you needed. I've had many friendships I thought would benefit me, but they backfired. Then I was back at ground zero. I found that every time one of my relationships ended, for the most part, it was for the best. I had learned all I could learn from that particular individual. At other times, the friendship was not what I needed on the path I needed to travel at that point.

> We catch what we put ourselves in position to catch.

The wrong people, if we allow them, can introduce needless detours and present roadblocks along our paths. We all need friends, but we must make sure we surround ourselves with the right people. Nobody has enough self-solitude to be alone 24/7. God put us on earth to unite and to be **ship**builders. According to Webster's dictionary, a *ship* is a vessel of some size adapted to navigation. Hence, the relationships, memberships, friendships, companionships, and so forth (friends) should help us navigate through life and not cause us to get off course. Friendships take time, understanding, and effort. You never know who your friends are until those times in your life when you need forgiveness, understanding, and a shoulder to lean on.

When we choose the wrong relationships, we pay a dear price! Good credit goes bad. A sound, melodious mind turns confused and noisy. A happy heart turns sorrowful! At times, I felt as if I was doing all the work in a friendship and was stressed because the other person did not care about the friendship as I did. This caused me to lose ground and weakened my identity. When you are losing ground because of stressful relationships, you can have your identity stolen! The Bible says, "He who walks with wise men shall be wise; but, a companion of fools will be destroyed" (Proverbs 13: 20 NKJV) and "Bad company corrupts good habits" (I Corinthians 15: 33 NKJV).

I wrote the following piece on the importance of a good relationship.

Catching Life

Today was a good day. I got up, prayed, went to church, and went to the park with my friend. My friend and I played catch with a baseball while we were there. While tossing the ball, I realized a truth behind playing catch.

*As I tossed him the ball and he tossed it back, we talked about things we wanted to accomplish in life. We had made it a habit to talk and share our dreams, aspirations, and goals. Although we did that often, today it seemed more powerful. Every time we threw the ball back and forth, my mind began to elevate to another level. It struck my spirit that **you'll only catch what you position yourself to catch.***

*From that point, I knew we were not simply throwing a ball to each other. Instead, we were throwing each other **encouragement, hope, inspiration, motivation, wisdom, and strength.** Every time we tossed that ball to one another, our conversation and friendship reinforced one another. See, we must realize we catch what we put ourselves in position to catch; and it mainly starts with the people with whom you surround yourself. For example, a match that is lit can light another match because it too has the potential to produce a flame. We must be* *around people who will light and ignite the fires within us.*

Who is your partner as you play catch over the course of life? Sometimes we play catch with people and receive negative things (foul balls) thrown our way. That's why we must watch with whom we catch because we're not just throwing a ball; instead, we're throwing life into another person. If someone isn't willing to speak life, wisdom, knowledge, and righteousness into your spirit, there's no reason you should be receiving what they're throwing to you. Remember, you will only catch what you open your glove to. In this case, the glove represents the mind. **The Bible says, "He who walks with wise men shall be wise. But, he who walks with fools will be destroyed" (Proverbs 13:20 NKJV).** *We are like sponges; we soak up what we saturate ourselves with.*

My friend and I wouldn't be able to catch today if we hadn't begun to seek the kingdom of God first. We are able to deposit into the life of the other because we are spiritually in tune. What we catch from the word of the Lord, we receive; and then we throw to each other for mutual encouragement.

The Bible also says, "A wise man will hear, and will increase learning; and a man of understanding will attain wise counsel"

(Proverbs 1:5 NKJV). We should always put ourselves opposite someone who's going to throw life into us. I'm not saying my friend and I are the smartest, the wisest, or the most educated. I'm simply suggesting that you should receive from someone who will speak life into you, whether it is your spouse, boyfriend, girlfriend, or just a friend. Make sure they're going to pass you something worth catching. So remember, if you catch anything at all, catch life!

At the end of day, relationship has a great deal to do with the person with whom we should engage in a game of catch. Remember, we have to walk through the valley of trust before we can reach the mountaintop.

When evaluating a relationship, or if you want to know if you've made the right choice for a relationship, ask yourself these questions:

- **Does this person make my life better or worse?** People who bring our lives into downward spirals are usually not the companions we need.

- **Does this person *add* to me or *subtract* from me?** There are people who sharpen, inspire, motivate, and affirm us. They are the people with whom we need to surround ourselves. We should hang around people who bring out the best in us simply because the people who bring out the worst in us can cause us to lose focus and our identities.

- **Does this person appreciate and respect me? Are they concerned with my best interests?** We should always have people around us who have our best interests. One of my biggest mistakes as a young man was choosing friends who could have cared less about this. People who are in your corner are the ones who will help you.

- **Does this person make personal sacrifices for me?** Friendships and relationships are two-fold. We are not to be strictly receivers or strictly givers. The relationship should have balance. We should not let people use us.

- **Does this person bring the best out of me?** I once heard a lady counselor say that when she was in high school and ran track, her coach purposely put her around people who could run faster than she to stretch and develop her ability. Likewise, we should associate with people who will push us. Once you expose yourself to someone on a higher level, it is hard to go back and be comfortable on the level where you began.

- **Can I make mistakes and still be accepted by this person?** We should also surround ourselves with people who know that mistakes are not fatal and will lift us back up when we fall. Good relationships help you through pain, not inflict more pain while you are down (talking behind your back).

- **Does this person inspire me to live a godly life?** Godly relationships are important. They provide a sense of accountability to live a life full of character, integrity, morals, and values. If we are constantly around people who don't keep us straight, we can veer off the path of purpose.

- **Does this person listen to me?** I once read that a friend will listen to your song and sing it back to you when you forget it. In a good relationship, the other person will listen to you when you need to vent and just be an ear. I fear those who always try to give advice and never take the time to listen. Listening means that the person hears your heart.

- **Does this person know how to correct me without tearing me down?** We should have people who know how to tell us the truth without putting us down. I've hung around plenty of people who let me have it, and they lowered my self-esteem and almost stole my purpose and identity. Although you may hear criticisms, never receive destructive words because everyone can change and improve.

- **Is this person physically, mentally, or verbally abusive?** Never put yourself in an abusive relationship, whether it is verbal, mental, or physical! Any type of abuse will lessen your confidence, cloud your purpose, and steal who you are as a person. You should cut off that type of relationship instantly.

- **Does this person dream?** We all need dreamers around us. They help us stay on our tiptoes so we don't become comfortable or mediocre. We should always strive to go above and beyond. If you have people who are around you with mediocre mindsets, they can rub off on you.

- **Does this person know his or her God-given purpose**? We should surround ourselves with people who have a sense of who they are destined to become. These people can help guide us in finding our purpose (if we don't know it already). Better yet, they can inspire us and make us accountable.

- **If this person leaves, will I be glad they're gone or sad they've left?** If people make the decision to walk out of our lives, we should let them keep going. We should never stress ourselves over people who are only meant to be there for a season.

You know the answers. Do what you have to do! If we make the wrong decisions in a relationship, we can suffer from loss of identity. Love them or leave them. You are worth the trip!

Growing up as a child, I watched my favorite cartoons and then tried to imitate what I had seen on the screen. My favorite was *Superman*. I loved the way he flew through the air and saved people. Nothing hurt him. I was so fascinated that I took sheets and tied them around my neck to be just like my superhero. I also watched action movies, imagining that I had the same abilities as the characters.

It's strange how we try to become the things that capture our hearts as small children. Nevertheless, today, we still have some adults who try to become the things they see that have captured their hearts. Many times these things have no place in the plans that God has for them, especially in adulthood.

I believe that trying to become what you behold instead of what you are created to be is one of the greatest enemies of the general population. Children and teenagers today often try to imitate actors, sports figures, and rappers. To young people, these individuals look as if they have all the power in the world. As children imitate these idols, they lose touch with what God created them to be. Instead, they start to create alternate personalities.

I've observed how even older men envy other men who are successful at attracting women or who drive nice cars and live in big houses. They try to imitate what they see in these men's lives as if that will fulfill them. I've also noticed women who try to glamorize themselves like supermodels to attract these same types of men.

Identity theft is all around when it comes to people not living who they are. I once heard a man say, "It's funny how we are all born originals, but most of us die as copies." We should strive to be the best persons we can possibly be. I'm not against having nice things but not at the expense of losing focus of our real identities. In our purpose, we find out who we really are. From that, all the other benefits will come.

I was born an original. God made no one else exactly like me. The same holds true for you. Because He saw fit to make me an original, I am determined not to die as a copy!

PROTECTION AGAINST THE ILLUSIONS OF PROSPERITY (Status) AND POSSESSIONS (Materialism)

"What you have or own is not who you are, but are the benefits from being who you are."
-Terence B. Lester

One of the greatest myths of life is that prosperity and possessions will make you happy. It is not my intent to indict prosperity or nice things unfairly, but they should never be the end products in acquiring happiness. In fact, I agree with having nice things; I don't agree with nice things having us. When I was laid off, I felt as if all I needed was a million dollars and all my problems would go away. I felt if I just could own what other individuals had then I would be all right. I thought that then I would not feel unhappy. I would not feel as if my whole world was about to collapse. However, even in my deepest despair, I knew that was not true.

> Possessions do not define who we are.

The purpose of this book is to inspire you to maintain a level of peace so that, when faced with any type of problem, nothing else matters because you are well aware of who you are and where you are headed in life. Despite the fact that many people equate what they have with who they are, in actuality, what they have is not enough to sustain them in the crises of life.

After being laid off, God brought a man into my life who weathered the storm with me. He was involved in real estate and was very successful financially. He helped me carry my bills, bought me a car, and helped to pay for my wedding. I knew this was nothing but the hand of God moving on behalf of His servant because I had the desire to serve Him with all my heart. When this happened, it really increased my faith and belief that God is always there with me. Some people get so wrapped up in what they have that they forget to acknowledge even the existence of God, let alone what He has done for them!

It is so important that we realize that possessions do not define who we are. God still deserves credit for that. My intention is never to allow achievement or certain levels of success interfere with acknowledging that He remains my source and continues to orchestrate the melodies of my life. I believe that because of doing what we're created to do, God will take care of everything else. Hence, the Bible encourages us to "seek first the kingdom of God and His righteousness and all things will be added." (Matthew 6:33 NKJV)

If we are not careful, the possessions and prosperity of life can and will rob us of our identities. There are many people who, when they become successful as athletes, actors, entertainers, lawyers, doctors, or other respected professionals, lose touch with humanity because they are too caught up in the recognition associated with their work.

Keeping Up With the Joneses

In college, all the guys and the ladies went shopping before school started and before special events such as parties and football or basketball games. I was always along with the group trying to buy the latest gear or shoes to show off. Although it was always nice shopping and getting new things, I found myself doing it for the wrong reasons. It was simply to keep up with everybody else. Some call it "keeping up with the Joneses."

American society seems to be on an endless quest either to out do or to out shine their neighbors. In doing so, we shop no longer for what we need but for what we feel will impress other people. I read that we buy things that we don't need to impress people that we don't like. Often we accumulate stuff and go years without ever using it again.

I want to reinforce that I'm in no way against buying new things or making quality purchases, but we should evaluate our motives. Whether we admit it or not, each one of us longs for attention and approval that only God can give. We long for people to affirm us and tell us how well we are doing or how good we are looking. We shun the thought of being in last place or feeling left behind. Many people go back to school to gain more degrees not because they don't have enough in life but because they don't want to feel inferior to those who already have high positions. Sometimes we misinterpret being in a blessed state:

- We are not blessed because we live in huge houses.

- We are not blessed because we have the choice of several nice cars in our possession.

- We are not blessed because we own Rolexes.

- We are not blessed because we have very fashionable wardrobes.

- We are not blessed because we have the money to have people serve our needs.

None of those are reasons within themselves to call ourselves blessed. All of these things are found as we search for the kingdom of God and operate in who we are created to be. We should consider ourselves blessed for circumstances that are more valid:

- We should call ourselves blessed because we know who we are in Jesus Christ.

- We should call ourselves blessed because we know why God created us and know He controls our destiny's course.

- We should call ourselves blessed because we know our place in the kingdom of God.

- We should call ourselves blessed because we know our purpose for being alive.

- We should call ourselves blessed because we can lead others to Christ and their destinies.

- We should call ourselves blessed because we don't blame anyone else for the mistakes we make.

- We should call ourselves blessed because we refuse to stay down when we are knocked down. (Even though blessed, you **will** be knocked down from time to time).

- We should call ourselves blessed because we have meaningful relationships with wise men and women of God.

- We should call ourselves blessed because we know how to repent for our sins.

- We should call ourselves blessed because others can benefit from our living.

At some point in life, we may be called upon to answer this simple question: "If everything that I have was taken away from me, then who would I be?"

If you had nothing and you were starting again in your life, no matter how successful or poor, who would you be? How would you find identity? Some people may read this material and say, "Well, I don't have a lot of money, and I don't have a big house." That is no excuse because that's exactly what I am trying to illustrate. What you have does not negate that you are created for a specific purpose.

> Each one of us longs for attention and approval that only God can give.

The Comparing Disease

The worst thing we can do while on the quest for purpose is addressed in a simple three-word phrase I heard from Bishop Dale Bronner, one of my favorite speakers: compare, complain, and compete. These words, which are deeply connected, can derail our identities. They can give birth to a condition I call "the comparing disease."

Whether we believe it or not, many times we analyze our level of success based upon another person's achievement. This can lead to a false sense of superiority because we may feel as though the people around us are not doing as well as we are. This artificially boosts our egos, which eventually causes harmful pride. On the other hand, we sometimes feel inferior because we perceive that we have accomplished less than people around us. Comparing, complaining, and competing can be detrimental to our total development. Refraining from these three habits can help us.

- **When you don't complain, you free yourself from negative thoughts**. When you participate, you also empower a world that says, "I can't."

- **When you don't compare, you free yourself from jealousy, envy, and inadequacy.** When you compare, you lose drive and feel as if you can't accomplish your dreams, purpose, or goals.

- **When you don't compete, you free yourself from doing stuff for others and not for God**. Don't force a blessing! When you do compete, you lose yourself.

Gratefulness

Some people are born into wealth and have millions from birth. This is a blessing. Yet some who don't have material wealth at all are still rich. No matter where we are in life, we should maintain a grateful spirit no matter what we own or possess. I've had to learn that happiness in life is all about how you see yourself in the midst of whatever circumstances you face.

After being laid off, my future wife and I wanted to do something to take our minds off the struggle. We gathered a lot of old things and headed to the downtown area. We were on a mission to locate people who were in worse positions than we were at the time. Finally, we came across a couple of people who were homeless, a lady and a gentleman. I stopped them and told them that my fiancée and I had some things we wanted to give them. Surprisingly, their faces lit up with joy. We gave them clothing and shoes that were old to us. They celebrated as if they had just won the lottery! It filled our hearts with joy to make someone else happy. We were blessed as we became a blessing to others despite what we were going through.

Wherever we are in life is always a great place to be. If we just look around, someone is in a worse situation. We can always find a reason to be grateful. Being grateful indeed has its own benefits:

1. **Gratefulness attracts positive attention.** Nobody wants to help a person with a bad attitude. When we learn to become grateful, God sends us blessings

through people. The man who helped my wife and me came into our lives because we were grateful.

2. **Gratefulness improves our relationships**. This helps us to see what we can learn from each other. There are times when we draw closer in our relationships with friends because we see their value and the ways they add to our lives.

3. **Gratefulness reduces negativity.** It is hard to be negative about our situations when we are thinking about things for which we are grateful. It is very hard not to be grateful that we have something to eat, no matter what it is, versus not having anything at all.

4. **Gratefulness improves problem-solving skills.** We learn how to solve problems once we go through them and grow through them. I heard a man say one time that "experience is not the only teacher; however, it is one of the best teachers."

5. **Gratefulness helps us to learn.** Every dark cloud has a silver lining. Behind every problem lies an opportunity. Being grateful for our situations, even if we don't like everything about them, allows us to be thankful for the opportunity to learn something new.

We should be grateful for everything that we possess, not allow those things to steal and rob us of why we are here on this earth. We should protect ourselves from the negative effects of prosperity and possessions.

PROTECTION AGAINST ARROGANT PRIDE AND PROGRESS

"A man wrapped in himself makes a very small bundle."
-Benjamin Franklin

Victim and Predator

I thought about these words one day, *victim* and *predator*. As I thought about both in depth, I found that there is a very thin line of distinction between the two. We can become victims by simply being in positions where we can be hurt by our families, associates, or friends. We can also be victims of various life circumstances or other problems. Many times, we can't control these situations. Fortunately, we can determine how we respond to them.

I also understand that many people fall victim to hurting others because they have been wronged. They feel life has not dealt them good hands. Consequently, they want to scramble someone else's deck. It's a principle that John Maxwell alludes to in his theory that "some hurt people, hurt people." They live the lives of both the victim and the predator.

The predator is one who is out to devour the prey. No matter the cost, predators will not be happy unless they have done their job of ruining others' situations. I believe that, as we all face circumstances, it is not how we react but how we respond that determines our outcomes.

I pray that today you will begin to see past the hurts of any individuals who may mistreat you or harm you and understand that we all are nothing without God. Instead of reacting irrationally, respond righteously!

I believe that negative pride erupts when we put our guard up too quickly, become arrogant about what we don't have to take, or think that everyone in the world owes us something. No matter what it is, pride can always be traced back to a past hurt or our upbringing. I am reminded of a simple wound and the scab that begins to form as the healing process begins.

The Scab and the Scar

Many times as I was growing up, I fell and received wounds from playing. I'm sure we all have. When you are wounded, the body automatically begins a healing process. However, it really is up to us how long the wound will take to heal.

One time in particular, I scraped my elbow playing football. After a couple of weeks, the wound created a scab but was not completely healed. After seeing the scab, I thought that it was healed; so I went right back out and played football. As I played, the scab came off and the wound was exposed again. The skin repair process had to begin all over, and the wound took longer to heal.

Here is the powerful truth that was revealed through this incident: If you've had certain things wound you in your past, you must take care of the wound so you can be healed of those things. If you do as I did, without healing fully, the scab may come off and you will take longer to heal.

After the wound has healed fully, you may have a scar. Scars are not always bad. If considered positively, they may build your testimony and help you heal others who have been wounded in a similar manner.

Your wounds may be relationships gone sour, divorces, job losses, mistreatment by your family, feelings of neglect, thoughts of why things are not happening for you, feelings of loneliness, or repeated failures. If any of those apply to you, know that your days ahead can be better.

Here are three things that will tell you if you still have a wound that requires total healing. **You have a wound if**

- New people (relationships) remind you of something that once hurt you, and you treat them as the past relationship instead of as a fresh encounter or opportunity.

- Circumstances that bothered you in the past bother you with the same intensity if you bring them up again.

- You become depressed sometimes just from thinking about your past.

Here are three things that indicate your wound has healed:

- You can use your experiences to help someone who is going through similar issues without getting hurt all over again.

- Your past does not hurt you at all when you think about it or bring it up.

- You are no longer depressed by your past.

It is just natural that as we move about the earth, at times we will receive wounds. Fortunately, God in His wisdom crafted a way for the body to be repaired and healed. Wounds, and consequently scars, are part of His total plan. He has a reason, time, and a season for all things. This reminds me of the great scripture passage in Ecclesiastes that refers to seasons and a purpose for all things. (Ecclesiastes 3:1)

> We all are nothing without God.

In Due Season

"For there is a time for everything, and a season for every activity under heaven" (Ecclesiastes 3:1 NIV). One of the most influential lessons we can learn is the greatness of nature and its seasons. Everything on earth has a season and a due course of events. In agriculture, there is a marked cycle of events associated with the seasons:

- Spring: sowing and growing
- Summer: harvest
- Autumn: breaking down
- Winter: rest

Every living thing has its own natural cycle of growth and rest. We grow and become great in similar ways:

- Seasons in our life for sowing and growing, the season of learning and purging.

- Seasons for harvesting, the season of increase.

- Seasons of breaking down, the season of process.

- Seasons of rest, the season of reflection

When we walk in the will of God, our lives will grow into greatness in due season. Seasons play a vital role in the production of fruit because, if issued at the wrong time, they aren't appreciated in the same light as if they are issued in proper order.

As in nature and agriculture, our lives reflect definite seasons:

- Children grow in due season and move out.

- Relationships grow in due season in trust and strength.

- Love grows to higher and higher levels.

- Wisdom grows to higher and higher levels.

- Experience grows in due season with proper investment of time and patience.

With the right amount of time invested into an area, something can grow to its maximum potential with the touch of God. We should think of our designated areas of greatness and of how we can work towards becoming great. We must ask ourselves, "Where am I in the season of personal development?"

- If it is spring, then we should sow and grow.

- If it is summer, then we should take advantage of the harvest.

- If it is autumn, we should break down that which doesn't serve us.

- If it is winter and we have performed all of the previous tasks, then we should take some time to rest, reflect, and rejuvenate.

Seasons and the consequent cycles of your life cannot move forward if you make the unfortunate decision to quit. Your seed will lie in the ground dormant, without the chance to germinate, take root, and grow. There will be no harvest. Whatever you do, don't give up and quit. Remember the poem that has become a source of encouragement for many, "Don't Quit."

Don't Quit

When things go wrong as they sometimes will,
When the road you're trudging seems all up hill,
When the funds are low and the debts are high
And you want to smile, but you have to sigh,
When care is pressing you down a bit,
Rest if you must, but don't you quit.
Life is queer with its twists and turns,
As every one of us sometimes learns,
And many a failure turns about
When he might have won had he stuck it out;

Don't give up though the pace seems slow—
You may succeed with another blow,
Success is failure turned inside out—
The silver tint of the clouds of doubt,
And you never can tell how close you are,
It may be near when it seems so far;
So stick to the fight when you're hardest hit—
It's when things seem worst that you must not quit.

-Unknown

THE **MAINTAINING OF YOUR PROTECTION**

~

"Consistency is the key to continual development."
-Terence B. Lester

Life is a process and improvement is ongoing. Even though we have definite purpose and possess individual identities, we should follow five basic steps to improve consistently upon what we have accomplished.

1. **See**: View the area in which you want to improve. This is the process of analyzing yourself.

2. **Plan**: Design strategies and activities to improve or develop in the desired area. This is the process of creating your blue print for attack.

3. **Do**: Implement strategies and activities into your life. This is the process of acting out what you've planned to accomplish.

4. **Check**: Analyze and review to see if everything seen, planned, and done has been implemented into your life. This is the process of checking to see if there has been change in your life.

5. **Repeat the process**: This step determines your consistency and willingness to improve.

Continual growth and improvement ultimately are determined by our abilities to remain diligent and faithful over a long period of time.

As we remain consistent, it is very important to stay in the lane in which God has planned for us to travel. For example, if your gifting is cooking, why be a mechanic? We must stay in our lanes and focus on what we are called to do. Sometimes when we try to do too much, we end up not accomplishing anything at all. We must have strategic focus, as I wrote about a few years ago in the following story.

Two Lanes

While on the expressway last night, I saw a car swerving in and out of lanes. As I passed and looked into the car, the driver seemed to be asleep. I politely honked the horn to wake him up before he caused a serious accident. I also noticed that he was driving down the middle of two lanes.

Driving down the middle of two lanes produces great danger. Falling asleep relinquishes control and can lead to going off track. Isn't it amazing that we can learn so much just from what we see!

As I rode past, I received great revelation! Spiritual messages began to flash before my eyes and into my spirit. The main revelation was, "Do not fall asleep at the wheels of life, stay in one lane, stay focused, and stay consistent. The moment you fall asleep, your focus will be diminished and you will be in position to cause great tragedy in your life."

Isn't it funny how at times we can be awake in life but asleep at the wheel? We can be right in the middle of causing great harm to others and ourselves because we are trying to do entirely too much. We are riding in two lanes, just as the man was in the vehicle.

*Normally, when we get out of our lanes of life and purpose, we have failed to make ourselves clear about what we are trying to achieve. The key word in the process is **focus**. Here are five things to let you know if you are not focused on your lane of destiny, which supports your identity:*

- *You're always changing your mind about your purpose.*

- *You're not clear on what you want.*

- *You're not around the people who will wake you before an accident.*

- *You are traveling in more than one lane.*

- *You are on the highway with no real destination.*

From this revelation, I learned that we should operate our lives in the proper lane and that we should remain alert and awake. I learned that our identity is dependent upon remaining focused and being in tune with what is going on around us.

> Continual growth and improvement ultimately are determined by our abilities to remain diligent and faithful over a long period of time.

SUMMARY

~

"Don't wait until everything is just right. It will never be perfect. There will always be challenges, obstacles and less than perfect conditions. So what. Get started now. With each step you take, you will grow stronger and stronger, more and more skilled, more and more self-confident and more and more successful."
-Mark Victor Hansen

We are exactly who God says we are! Nothing else matters. We must work to safeguard our identities by acknowledging that we accept His designation. We must not be influenced by circumstances or individuals who strive to change our God-ordained designations. We spend much of our lives trying to protect ourselves against fraud and evil. Yet, the worst evil sneaks into our lives like a thief in the dark.

God has created us to be the head and not the tail, above and not beneath, blessed and not cursed. Sometimes, we are not watchful and allow the enemy to convince us otherwise. We are granted authority so that we can rule and reign. Does it make any sense to have such privilege and forfeit the entire benefit package? That's exactly what identity theft does.

God thought enough of us to make us in His own image. This in itself says much. We submit needlessly to abuse, neglect, condemnation, low self-esteem, and alienation simply because we allow circumstances or individuals rob us of the identities that God gave us in the Garden of Eden. It was here that He gave man dominion over all things in the earth. It is sad that, after such privileges were given to Adam, he was tempted and fell prey to a lowly force that comes only to **steal** identity, **kill** identity, and **destroy** identity!

Just like Jesus, we will be tempted along the way to have second thoughts about who we are or who we can become. There will be times when other people will openly question who we are or start rumors that totally contradict the identity designations we have been given. Unfortunately, the Internet has become an open forum for destruction and distortion of personal identities.

We must remember several things as we maintain a special place in Him to preserve our identities:

1. We must resort to the same tactics that He uses and **rebuke** negative influences. We can do this by using God's Word against the enemy. We must protect ourselves in relationships, the actions we take, and the attitudes we display.

2. We must form our own encouragement society so that, during those times that circumstances are negative, we will still persevere.

3. We must acknowledge and thank the Creator for His mercy and grace in our lives. We must never assume that we are solely responsible for gifts, talents, and accomplishments.

4. We must wrap our lives and endeavors in prayer.

5. We must walk as though we have been called for His purpose.

6. We must anticipate destiny with a spirit of humility and praise.

7. We must lock certain protective measures in our spirits and build walls to prevent the following from negative intrusion (to name a few):

    - Our past
    - Unforgivingness
    - Lack of focus
    - Excuses
    - Devaluation
    - Obstacles (inflicted by individuals and circumstances)
    - Complaints
    - Curse words
    - Procrastination
    - Self-serving philosophy, power, and position
    - Wrong associations

Finally, I cannot emphasize enough that identity is a precious personal possession. In all instances, we must watch over our identities and prevent opportunities for them to be stolen. Both maintenance and control lie within our hands. We must acknowledge them; appreciate them; cultivate them; control them; and most of all, **thank God for them!** He could have given our identities to someone else!

My prayer is that you can discern how we fall into traps hidden along life's paths. There is an old song found in some hymnals, "Somewhere Listening for My Name." This is the first line: "When He calls me, I will answer." The question is do **you** know your real name? You are not what the world has labeled you. Rather, you are who God has called you to be. His promises are "yea" and "amen." He is your support and your guide. It was never His intention that you become a floor mat for the world to walk on or to ridicule and ultimately convince you that you are not His child. There are rights that come with being a part of His family!

Recently, a man took the name of one of the richest families in America. He managed to gain entry into many places just by using this prestigious false alliance. He bought properties, married, impressed his neighbors, gained employment, and traveled near and far based on the identity of this well-established name. A criminal act brought the entire matter to a screeching halt. By this time, however, he had done much damage, deceived a wife, fathered a child, abducted the child, and deceived many other people. He stole the name and gained as much mileage as possible for as long as he could continue to operate as an imposter.

Now, just think what you and I can accomplish under the real banner and authority of the Lord Jesus Christ! We are protected and covered by the most powerful and prestigious name in the universe—Jesus Christ, Lord of Lords, King of Kings! We belong to Him!

Before we finish, I want to lead you in a confession of salvation. This special privilege opens the door to **all** of His promises and provides assurance for the believer. The Bible tells us in 2 Corinthians 5:17 (NKJV), "Therefore, if anyone is in Christ, he is a new creation; old things have passed away; behold, all things have become new." That verse is simply saying once we accept Jesus Christ as our personal savior, we will become new creations with totally new identities in God through His Son. If we truly want to receive these God-given identities or maintain our identities, we must constantly confess and believe we are Christ's seed. In Romans 10:9-10 (NKJV), the Bible tells us "[9]that if you confess with your mouth the Lord Jesus and believe in your heart that God has raised Him from the dead, you will be saved. [10]For with the heart one believes unto righteousness, and with the mouth confession is made unto salvation." It is simply saying that before you can receive a new identity in God through Christ, you must accept Jesus as your savior. I have included a simple prayer you may use to receive your new identity. This is **the ultimate invitation**.

Prayer for Salvation

Dear Heavenly Father,

Thank You for sharing your identity with me. Thank You so much for making me in Your image. Thank You for caring enough about me that You sent Your Son to die on the cross so that condemnation would not be a part of my legacy.

Thank You for forgiving me of my sins, each one of them. Thank You that You are with me every step of the way. Please help me not to be afraid of what the world says about me. Help me to trust Your word and accept my position in You.

Thank You for giving me an identity that the world cannot redefine. Thank You for keeping my eyes on You through every trial and set of circumstances that may come against me.

Lord, I now give my life fully to You. I am Your child. I am willing to walk with You forever.

In the name of Jesus,

Amen!

P.S. God bless you and may God allow you to walk strong in your new identity.

ABOUT THE AUTHOR

~

Terence B. Lester was born in Atlanta, Georgia, on December 4, 1982. He is the son of Tyrone Lester and Connie Walker and has one younger sister, Ashley Lester. He has a wonderful supportive wife, Cecilia L. Lester, who aids him with his speaking and writing. They have a beautiful daughter, Zion Joy Lester, who is the apple of their eyes. He is an anointed "Moses" of the 21st century! He has dedicated his life to mentoring young people and young adults as they are forced to make tough decisions in a difficult world.

This 26-year-old man has lived through peril, trial, disappointment, and now jubilation! He has emerged a powerful, dynamic spokesperson ably equipped to address an entire generation. Unfortunately, the voices of parents often go unheard. Their repeated messages become constant. Their pleas for conformity often fall on deaf ears.

Lester earned a bachelor of theology degree from Atlanta Bible College and serves as a willing Christian mediator. He is **for** both sides; he understands misguided youth and empathizes with troubled parents. According to this high-energy crusader, "There **is** an oasis in the middle of this wilderness experience!" With fresh memories of a turbulent childhood, he is destined to help young people and young adults avoid traps that become deadly as each day goes by. His goal is to bring young people and their parents to meaningful points of understanding and agreement. Although it sounds like an impossible dream, it has become reality for Terence, his mother, his wife, and those who have prayed for him over many years. Now he is a much sought-after speaker and facilitator of youth group sessions and conferences. He is also a recognized poet and a prolific writer.

A devout Christian and follower of Jesus Christ, Lester reminds the world that there is absolutely **nothing** too hard for God! Because God has planted in Lester a burning desire to lead young people out of a modern-day Egypt, he has no doubt that the same God will prove faithful and use him to continue to share a message of love, hope, reconciliation, healing, and divine destiny to thousands.

Equipped with prayer and an unusual ability to relate to his audience, Lester stands boldly before young people not as another religious leader but as a child of God with a fresh application and covering of the blood of Jesus each time he stands before a group. It takes only moments for them to realize that this young man is **real**!

Lester comes not to challenge prior Christian teaching or diminish parental influence. Rather, he comes to augment and make plain that which has been spoken. Until the message is understood and until it has been received, it may as well not have been delivered at all! He has come to stand in partnership and agreement with those who love God and are unwilling to give up on young people.

Our youth **deserve** the chance to sit at the feet of this ex-juvenile delinquent, ex-drug user, former thief, ex-gang member, and a defiant son. They deserve the chance to see what God has done in his life. They will have to see the changed man to believe it! They need to meet and touch a man who has definitely made a U-turn.

Prepare to receive letters of testimony and thanks after this young man has had the opportunity to minister to a confused generation wandering in an even more confused world!

If you have been praying to God for ways to impact your young people spiritually— sons, daughters, or one young person in particular—then Terence B. Lester is part of your answer! Hear ye him!

Contact Information

Terence Lester is available for speaking engagements, book signings, workshops, and conference participation. Please submit details to the following address:

>Terence Lester
>PO BOX 1376
>Red Oak, GA, 30272

To book engagements, please send the following information:

- Date and length of event

- Contact person

- Contact information (phone, fax, email address)

- Event type (conference, ministry engagement-church service, youth service, panel participant, etc.)

- Target audience (church congregation, mixed ages, youth service, young adults, etc.)

- Venue (actual size of engagement)

You may go online and request Terence Lester's services or books on the World Wide Web.

>Website: www.terencelester.com
>Email Address: contact@terencelester.com
>Phone: 404-606-3116 or 770-875-3462

Thanks for your support!

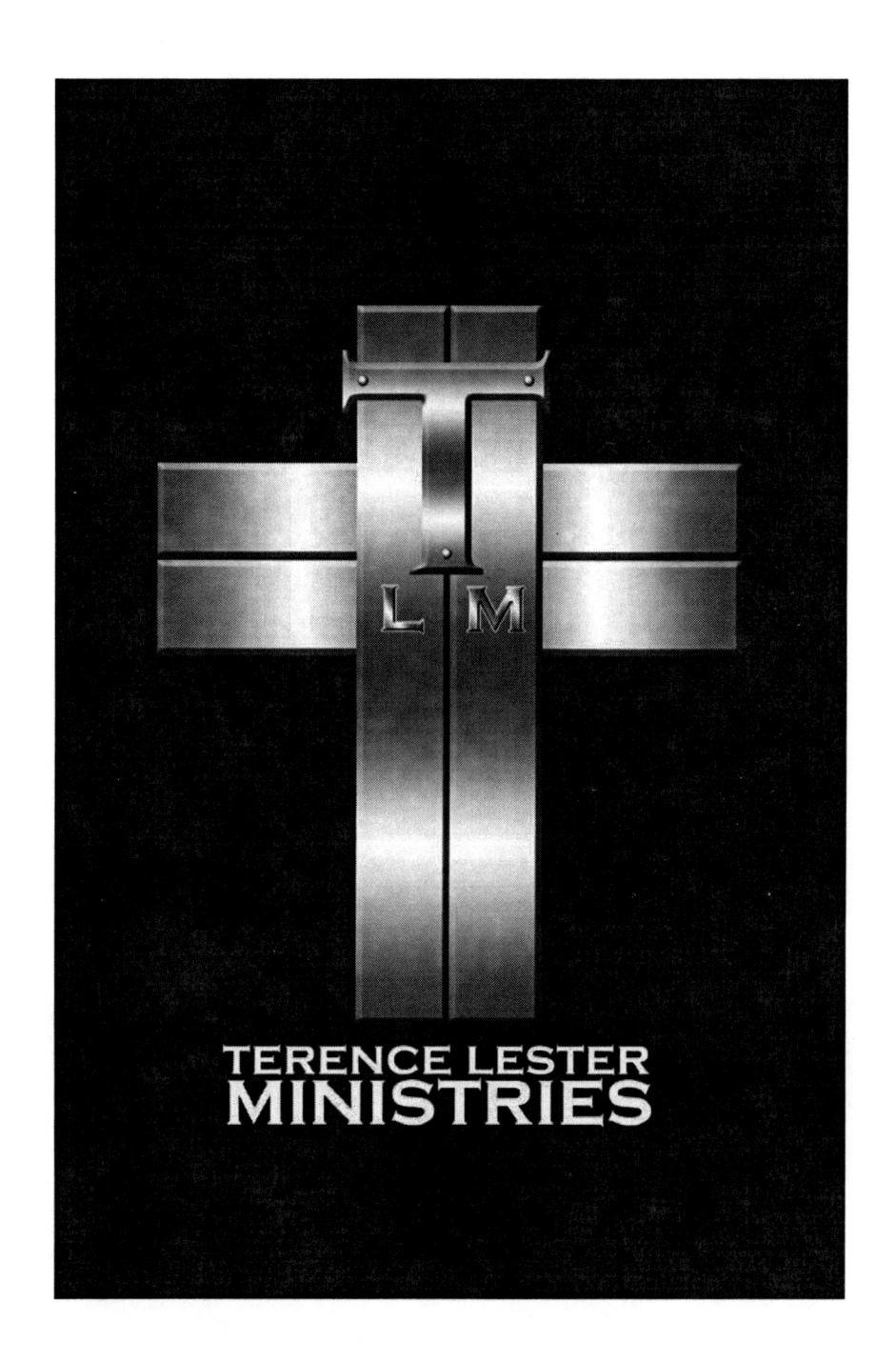

TERENCE LESTER MINISTRIES

Made in the USA